LOVE'S DRUM

ALSO BY PIR ELIAS AMIDON

Earth Prayers: 365 Prayers, Poems,
and Invocations from Around the World
(Elizabeth Roberts, co-editor)

Honoring the Earth: A Journal of New Earth Prayers
(Elizabeth Roberts, co-editor)

Life Prayers: 365 Prayers, Blessings, and
Affirmations to Celebrate the Human Journey
(Elizabeth Roberts, co-editor)

Prayers for a Thousand Years
(Elizabeth Roberts, co-editor)

The Open Path: Recognizing Nondual Awareness

Free Medicine: Meditations on Nondual Awakening

Munajat: Forty Prayers

The Book of Flashes

LOVE'S DRUM

Sufi Views, Practices, and Stories

Pir Elias Amidon

SENTIENT PUBLICATIONS

A paperback original

Cover design by Kim Johansen, Black Dog Design, www.blackdogdesign.com

Library of Congress Cataloging-in-Publication Data

Names: Amidon, Elias, author.

Title: Love's drum : Sufi views, practices, and stories / Pir Elias Amidon.

Description: First. | Boulder : Sentient Publications, LLC, 2023. | Summary: "A collection of short pieces about the Sufi path. The Sufi path is not limited to being "the mystical dimension of Islam", as Sufism is typically described. Sufism is an open path, inclusive, experiential, and non-definitive. It has no dogma or doctrine. It honors all human attempts to express the inexpressible, no matter what religious tradition they arise within"— Provided by publisher.

Identifiers: LCCN 2023011716 (print) | LCCN 2023011717 (ebook) | ISBN 9781591813057 (trade paperback) | ISBN 9781591813064 (ebook)

Subjects: LCSH: Sufism. | Sufism—Anecdotes.

Classification: LCC BP189.5 .A45 2023 (print) | LCC BP189.5 (ebook) | DDC 297.4—dc23/eng/20230414

LC record available at https://lccn.loc.gov/2023011716

LC ebook record available at https://lccn.loc.gov/2023011717

Printed in the United States of America

10 9 8 7 6 5 4 3 2 1

SENTIENT PUBLICATIONS
A Limited Liability Company
PO Box 1851
Boulder, CO 80306
www.sentientpublications.com

*This book is dedicated to
the vision of the Beloved Community*

Contents

PRACTICES

STORIES

Foreword

In this delightful book Sufi teacher Pir Elias Amidon reveals the Great Give-Away, the Free Medicine of pure awareness that's constantly present, effortlessly available, that frees our mind and quenches our soul, by inviting us into an unbounded matrix of pure selfless love.

In his magical prose Elias writes from the same mystical reverie that inspired the poetry of nondual mystics like Ibn 'Arabi and Longchenpa. In this sweet evocation of essays and practices, Elias gently unwinds the linear logic of our dualistic mind and reveals the ineffable, ungraspable presence of awareness itself.

With the undaunting exuberance that's the signature of Elias's spoken and written words he sweeps away the self-pitying dramas of our life, nurturing in their place a love that blossoms in our heart, and which comes to full bloom as the essenceless essence of divinity itself.

Each of us, though centerless and unfindable, is a crucible of sourceless love — love that can transmute the energies of conflict and pointless destruction into a heaven on earth where everything exists in the truth of its own unique, divine radiance. Within the cathedral of our minds lies a bliss-field of galactic magnitude and unfathomable glory that transcends life and death, pleasure and pain, and time and space.

In these pages Elias reveals the alchemy of nondual freedom. He unfolds the possibility of transfiguring our bounded and limited lives into lives of undefended love and generosity. In an arc of cosmic dimensions, Elias unites the mundane concerns of daily life and the transcendent reality of deity herself.

If you haven't yet had an opportunity to hear the freshness and vitality of Elias's spoken words, I encourage you to meet him in person, or through his recorded sharings. In the meantime, you can saturate your soul with the love and wisdom in these pages. By reading and reflecting on Elias's words you will enter a realm in which nondual awareness reveals the intricate beauty of our own incarnation.

DR. PETER FENNER
Author of *Radiant Mind*
and *Natural Awakening*

Author's Note

THIS LITTLE BOOK IS ABOUT LOVE. The views, practices, and stories recounted here, each in their own way, try to reflect a fragment of love's mystery and how it can enlighten this not-always-easy human journey we're on.

As I wrote these short pieces over the past five years for students and others interested in the Sufi path, I often felt I was holding a little mirror up to the world and in that shimmering piece of reflected light there appeared to me a glint of love's boundless and ineffable reality. Attempting to put those glints of light into words has been an almost impossible task, probably because words, no matter how poetic and elegantly arranged, cannot help but stop short of the intimacy that is the nature of love.

Love's intimacy is your and my most intimate place, the very gift of our being. It's what gives us, to be, now. It holds us, sustains us, and opens each moment into the next. It gives everything, everywhere. It hums every atom and swirls every galaxy. It's what unites us with all being and becoming, and yet no matter how vast and inconceivable love is, it's still the most intimate nature of our present experience. How curious it is that its wondrous nature is so close while it remains forever beyond the reach of words! Love's drum uses a deeper sound.

What I understand as "Sufism" is also beyond the reach of words, though many have certainly tried. This may be because, as the eleventh century Sufi Abdullah Ansari suggests, Sufism is simply another word for love. As will be obvious in these pages, the Sufi path I follow is not limited to being "the mystical dimension of Islam," as Sufism is typically described. To me, Sufism is an open path, inclusive, experiential, and non-definitive. It has no dogma or doctrine. It honors all human attempts to express the inexpressible, no matter what religious tradition they arise within. As Ibn 'Arabi famously says it, *"I profess the religion of love. Wherever its caravan turns along the way, that is the belief, the faith I keep."*

My deepest hope is that here and there within these essays you may catch a glimpse of love's divine wonder, or perhaps hear in your heart the intimate beat of its drum.

VIEWS

The History of Love

As THE STORY GOES, 13.77 BILLION years ago the universe was born from a "point" of near-infinite temperature and gravity, a point described as a "singularity" appearing before time and space had any meaning. And then, whoosh! from this impossible-to-comprehend singularity the entire universe of energy-matter expanded in all directions, which it apparently keeps on doing even now. Yet as it expands there's another movement — the energy-matter obeys a call of mutual attraction, a drawing to-gether into stars, galaxies, planets, and us wondering about it all.

One of the things we wonder about is the nature of these two "forces" of expansion and attraction — what are they? what moves them? The "whoosh" emerging from the singularity — what propels it into becoming? And conversely, this attraction — what causes it? *What's inside the "wish" of isolated particles to come closer, to draw together into stars and planets, you and me?* We've named that wish "gravity." Astrophysicist Brian Swimme calls it *allurement* — a sexy word for something so vast!

The whoosh and the wish — let's play with these words — the whoosh is the divine, holy *halleluiah!* and the wish is its desire for intimacy and connection. The whoosh in the Quran is Allah's universe-creating decree — *kun faya kun* — *Be! and it is!* and the wish is Allah's statement overheard by Mohammed, *"I was a hidden treasure and I loved to be known. Hence I created the world so that I would be known."* The whoosh in Buddhism is the light-body of the Buddha called the *sambhogakaya;* the wish is the Buddha-body of everything we see around us, the *nirmanakaya.* In Christian mysticism the whoosh is the flight of the Holy Spirit everywhere, and the wish the incarnation of Christ as the world.

All these metaphors — a singularity, a Big Bang, *Be! and it is!* Buddha bodies, Holy Spirit, Christ, the love to be known — ultimately they're all poetry, flinging us into a wordless space where we might glimpse what we're made of, what calls us, and what guides us.

From this perspective we witness the history of the universe revealing both the forces of unimaginable generosity — the whoosh — *Here! a universe for you!* — and the desire within it — the wish — toward connection, inter-relation, intimacy. Generosity — the gift of *becoming*; intimacy — the joy of *communion.*

What can we call this but *love?*

The history of the universe is the history of love. We can feel how the universe's love story is alive in our own experience, in the feelings of expansiveness and intimacy that simultaneously appear in our hearts when we love. We might think these are strictly personal feelings, our own good luck, but in fact they're the life of the whole universe as it comes into being. As above, so below. As everywhere, so here.

I realize this vision of a universe made of love may seem like wishful thinking, especially as we witness in our time so much selfishness and injustice, and so much of the beauty and life of our planet being destroyed.

But it is not a hoped-for vision. It's evident in the history of the universe, in its boundless generosity and its desire for communion. We're made of it. We're made of its generous and intimate love. Knowing this is true, not just intellectually but in our bones, in how we experience our *becoming* moment by moment, can give us the courage to carry on, no matter what happens. The force — of the entire universe! — is with us.

Human Being

HOW MARVELOUS THIS CREATURE, *the human being!* What a wonder and privilege it is to be one!

I know it doesn't always seem that way — we humans can be vicious and cruel, short-sighted, selfish, and petty — so to say that we're marvelous can sound naïve. But in this strange, nervous, pandemic time when we've had to pull back from close contact and have become so wary of each other, perhaps it would do us good to remember, for a moment, the miracle at the heart of what a human being is.

This miracle is a constant theme in Sufi teachings and poetry. Ibn 'Arabi, the great thirteenth century Sufi mystic and metaphysician, described the human being as a *barzakh*, an "isthmus." Human-being is an isthmus between the seeming polarities of matter and spirit, body and soul, the dense and the subtle. Like the Isthmus of Panama, where the vast continents of North and South America meet, the isthmus that is human beingness is "the Towering Station" amongst all *barzakhs*. Ibn 'Arabi:

The barzakh *is between-between,*
a station between this and that,
not one of them, but the totality of the two.
It has the towering exaltation,
the lofty splendor,
and the deep-rooted station.

This is what Rumi calls *"the majesty that lives in the deep cen-ter of everyone."* I suspect it is a majesty that lives in the deep center of everything, in the tree and the mountain, the rabbit and the hawk, but in the *barzakh* of *human being* it can be known, and once known it becomes a source of wisdom and loving kind-ness. Rumi:

You are a joining point of sky and ground,
soul as witness, green compassion.

The binary name *human being* itself reveals the miraculous *barzakh* we are. *Human* is a word derived from *humus*, earth, — the human is an earthling. Our extraordinarily complex and wondrous bodies are born of the earth — skin, bone, blood, and brain — a living system of matter and energy. The second part of our name, *being*, points to the ineffable quality of the creature we are: call it *spirit*, or *presence*, or *awareness*. Our nature of *being awareness* cannot be objectified in the way our earthling bodies can. Together, the two words suggest the *barzakh* we are: *human-being* — "a station between this and that, not one of them, but the totality of the two."

It's fairly easy to sense this in the moment: first you can know yourself as body, manifested as the sensuous organism of matter that you are, *and* you can know yourself as a locus of awareness, an ineffable presence, clear and ungraspable. You are *human, being.* An isthmus "between" matter and spirit, it is in this "Towering Station" that the seeming duality of matter and spirit can be recognized as not-two. As Rumi invites us:

> *Come out here where the roses have opened.*
> *Let soul and world meet.*

This is the miracle of *human-beingness.* In the place of meeting, in what Rumi calls "the spirit-form we are," a wondrous alchemy becomes possible. Our spirit-being enlightens our earthling-nature, and our earthling-nature gives clear spirit a field of sensate beauty and impermanence in which to love and play, become attached, suffer, and with any luck, recognize "the towering exaltation" within which it arises.

One of the most profound and beautiful expressions of this earth-spirit-human-being miracle can be found in the concluding passage of Rilke's *Ninth Elegy.* Here, in Stephen Mitchell's translation, Rilke is praising to the angels the "Things" of the earth, and reveals how they become "invisible" in us, in our love and amazement and gratitude:

> *...And these Things,*
> *which live by perishing, know you are praising them;*
> *transient,*

they look to us for deliverance: us, the most transient of all.
They want us to change them, utterly, in our invisible heart,
within—oh endlessly—within us! Whoever we may be at
last.

Earth, isn't this what you want: to arise within us,
invisible? Isn't it your dream
to be wholly invisible someday?—O Earth: invisible!
What, if not transformation, is your urgent command?
Earth, my dearest, I will. Oh believe me, you no longer
need your springtimes to win me over—one of them,
ah, even one, is already too much for my blood.
Unspeakably I have belonged to you, from the first.
You were always right, and your holiest inspiration
is our intimate companion, Death.

Look, I am living. On what? Neither childhood nor future
grows any smaller ... Superabundant being
wells up in my heart.

So Close

From the Tibetan Shangpa Kagyu tradition comes this exquisite riddle:

> *It's so close you can't see it.*
> *It's so profound you can't fathom it.*
> *It's so simple you can't believe it.*
> *It's so good you can't accept it.*

What is it?

The wonderful thing about this riddle is that it's compounded of paradox — pure positivity (so close, so profound, so simple, so good) and pure negativity (you can't see it, you can't fathom it, you can't believe it, you can't accept it). It's saying that no matter how we look for, or what we call this "it," it escapes the looking and the telling.

In most texts these lines are not referred to as a riddle but are given the whimsical title: "the four faults of awareness." But if we think "awareness" is the answer to the riddle, we've missed the point. To say "awareness" is to make a conceptual conclusion, and whatever this "it" is, it's neither bounded like a conclusion nor objective like a concept. Yes, the lines are referring to awareness, but do we really get what that is, beyond the idea that the word "awareness" represents? The beauty of the riddle is that it forces us to the edge of language and then pushes us off.

Although these four lines certainly cannot be improved, I'd like to offer a few thoughts here in the hope they may help, in some small way, with that push.

It's so close you can't see it

One way to enter the mystery of this line is to imagine space. Space is close and invisible too. It's extraordinary, isn't it, that we can have a sense of space without being able to see or feel it? Our bodies move through space and though space doesn't separate to let us by, we feel no resistance — it goes right through us. Whatever our riddle is referring to *is that close.*

The great nondual teacher Jean Klein says it's our "nearest." So near it has no distance to travel to get any nearer. Sufis prize "nearness to God" and mean the same thing. "I am closer to thee than thy jugular vein," it says in the Quran. In this case the words "close" and "near" are not about location or distance — they refer to identity, being so close to it we *are* it.

And so it is with our awareness. Can we find anything nearer to us than awareness? It's so close we can't see it, just like the eye cannot see the eye. Awareness is not seeable, though it is self-evident. And though the analogy of awareness being "like space" may be helpful, unlike our sense of space, awareness cannot be measured.

It's so profound you can't fathom it

This line drops the bottom out. It says we simply cannot understand what this is. To say it's "awareness" doesn't take us very far, since no one has ever fathomed awareness. Mystics have continually pointed out that awareness is the ground of all being, and now physicists are beginning to discover the same thing. But to say this is not to fathom it — it simply provides another mysterious description. This that we're speaking of cannot be fathomed. It is a mystery and will remain that way because it cannot be focused into an object that our minds can surround. *Mysterium profundum!* The Divine Unknown.

To the extent we can admit this, humility graces our being. Our drive to understand, our insistence on possessing this profundity with our intellects… relaxes. The mind surrenders, making way for something we might call devotion, love, gratitude, or praise.

It's so simple you can't believe it

What it is is so simple that it can't provide any kind of story or concept for us to believe in. Every word we use passes right through it. Plotinus calls it "the One" — that which is uncompounded, that has no predicate, the absolutely simple first principle of all. Buddhists call it emptiness. Sufis call it the void of pure potential.

Does its primal simplicity mean we cannot experience it? We can, but not as an experience. To open to this non-experience we must ourselves become simple. We must become transparent to ourselves.

> *In the uncertain light of single, certain truth,*
> *Equal in living changingness to the light*
> *In which I meet you, in which we sit at rest,*
> *For a moment in the central of our being,*
> *the vivid transparence that you bring is peace.*
> — *Wallace Stevens, from "Notes Toward a Supreme Fiction"*

Becoming transparent is not so difficult as it sounds, since our true nature is already transparent. It is the transparence of pure presence — or as some call it, presence-awareness. If we try to picture pure presence, we can't. If we try to fathom it, we can't. If we try to believe in it, we miss it — it's simpler than anything we can approach through belief.

And yet it's here, the simple pure presence of being, vividly immanent every moment in how everything appears, while at the same time transcending every appearance, every moment.

It's so good you can't accept it

This final line may be the most mysterious of all. We might think that if something is really good we could easily accept it, but the goodness this line points to is beyond the capacity of our acceptance. We cannot contain it — our *"cup runneth over."*

We have come to believe that this reality we're in is a tough place. We're threatened by illness, violence and death. Everything that we have will one day be taken away. How could the truth be something so good that it both holds and supersedes our pain and grief? The stubbornness of that question is one reason why we can't accept this that is "so good."

As in the preceding lines, "accepting it" hits the same limits that seeing, believing, and fathoming run into. As long as we think there is something we have to do — seeing, believing, fathoming, or accepting — we will miss what this is about.

This that is *so good* pervades all being. It is the pure love-generosity that is so close, so profound, so simple we can't surround it with our usual ways of knowing and feeling. As Rumi advises, *"Close these eyes to open the other. Let the center brighten your sight."*

Impermanence and Love

A LITTLE CHILD RUNS ACROSS THE lawn into her mother's waiting arms. The mother cuddles the child and makes cooing sounds, and then the little one slips off her lap and races around the yard again, tumbling and showing off.

That was many years ago. Now the child no longer exists; a grown-up person has taken her place. The mother is no longer waiting with her arms open. She, too, no longer exists.

This is the hard truth of impermanence, and it's how we usually think of that word — the endings it forces on us, the goodbyes, the losses and poignancy of *never again*.

The old Buddhists tell us the nature of impermanence is ultimately unsatisfactory. I imagine that's doubly true if you believe we've had countless lives before this one, all of them marked by the losses we've endured. We come here, we get attached to these beautiful bodies, to our loved ones, to the places and activities we love, and then they change and disappear. Impermanence tears at our attachments and makes *dukha*, suffering — this is the reason they say impermanence is "unsatisfactory."

Of course, impermanence doesn't work only at the level of human attachment and suffering. If we look closely at the fine-grain of our experience, we can see impermanence acting in every instant and in every place. Each moment yields to the next and never returns. The events we are experiencing right now — physical, thoughtful, emotional — have already changed. You breathe. Your attention moves. Your body shifts. Appearances arise and vanish. Nothing stays the same.

We might think that "I" stay the same through all this change — but what is this "I" that stays the same? When I look closely at the evidence of the moment, at the point-instant of transience, what kind of "I" is really there?

Looking directly at impermanence like this is not easy. But when we can manage it, when we can look clearly at the transient nature of our experience, that recognition naturally floods back into us and erases our sense of being something *outside* of transience, something substantial and separate. As an early Buddhist scripture reports the Buddha saying:

> In one who perceives impermanence, the perception of nonself becomes firmly established; and one who perceives nonself achieves the elimination of the conceit "I am" and attains nirvana in this very life.

And in the words of the Quran: "Everything is perishing except God's Face."

God's Face, nirvana — what are these scriptures pointing to? By perceiving the continuous flow of impermanence (the perishing), the conceit of our isolated selfness is washed away. But we don't vanish, just as the universe doesn't vanish because of the impermanent nature of each moment. What's holding everything together? What *isn't* perishing?

This is where the deeper secret of impermanence is revealed. As we come face-to-face with the fact that everything is perishing, that our lives and all appearances are thoroughly ephemeral, the realization of what's called "nonself," or "emptiness," or "openness" is born. In that realization we sense, beyond our senses, something that resists all description, something that we might variously call *God's Face*, or *nirvana*, or *holy intimacy*, or simply, *love*.

Whatever we call it, *this-that-does-not-perish* is what connects us with everything — each other, the trees, the mountains, the sky, the stars, and all beings who have ever appeared. We remain the unique beings we are, but we recognize we're not alone in our beingness, we are *with* the entirety.

I think of this "with-ness" as *love* — love that's both complete in itself and endlessly creative, a *holy intimacy* that is cosmic, inconceivable, awesome, and at the same time ordinary, everyday, and particular. It's the primordial generosity and ecstasy of light flooding the universe, and it's the energy of the little child running to her mother.

Of course, impermanence is painful for us too — there's no way we can escape loss and grief since everything we have ever been given in this life we will lose. But our grief too is love, it's the form love takes when great loss comes to us, the cry of *with-ness* as it breaks free from particular love into universal love.

Knowing this doesn't avoid the sorrow that impermanence visits upon us, but it embraces it in a larger order. People, things, and experiences come and go, but the truth of our connectedness is the reality that doesn't.

The Tree of Awe

ABOVE THE ALTAR IN THE CHAPEL at Nada Hermitage — a small Carmelite place of retreat in the Colorado desert — hangs a crucifix unlike any I have ever seen. It almost speaks. Jesus is clearly alive there, nailed to his cross of wood. His chest swells forth, almost grotesque, as if his heart is about to burst out of its confines. His face is turned, looking slightly away and up, with an expression of such surprise and awe that you imagine the sky has broken open with a supernal light that only he can see.

The symbology of this icon may be extreme, but for me it speaks exactly of our condition, each of us, here on earth. For who among us can escape tragedy, agony, loss, and heartbreak? Even those with seemingly delightful, easy lives must experience the death of loved ones, the poignancy of things passing, and witness the unhealable anguish suffered by our brothers and sisters throughout the world. It breaks our hearts. All of us live with broken hearts, whether from the great disappointment we feel for our species' repeated descents into violence and meanness, or from smaller, but no less intense, disappointments we feel for not being loved the way we want, or for not being the person we hoped to be, or for not being understood, or for any of our countless dreams deferred. When we do experience sweet moments of love and intimacy, it doesn't take long before things change and we get irritable or feel pressured and the sweetness is gone. That's heartbreak too. We can't avoid it, just like Jesus can't avoid his cross.

Sufis speak of a timeless time when "we were what we were before we were," a time of pure unity when there was no division between us and the Absolute. But then a line was drawn that allowed there to be lover and beloved. Loverness and belovedness searched for each other, seeking their unity, but even when they succeeded, the union could not last. "If there is pain," wrote the 17th century Indian Sufi Kwaja Khurd, "it is this: This state [of unity] cannot be permanent, since it has been established that the self-disclosure of the Essence passes like a flash of lightning and does not remain. O the infinite pain, the endless agony!"

That, too, is our heartbreak, at least for those of us mystically inclined. Jesus' body on that cross seems to want to fly free toward the light, but is nailed there, caught.

And yet there is something else alive for us in this polarity of heartbreak and joy, separation and unity — the vertical and horizontal axes of the cross. In a couplet written by Jelaluddin Rumi, the secret within the meeting of these two opposites is expressed:

You must have shadow and light source both.
Listen, and lay your head under the tree of awe.

The first line states the irrevocable nature of the cross we bear: we *must* have shadow and light both. There is no way out of it here on earth. And then the second line begins with two instructions: "listen" and "lay your head under." We might think Rumi would use the word "see" rather than "listen," since shadow and light are visual images, but the event of listening asks a greater surrender, an emptying out, a receiving. We lay our head under and stop trying to think our way through this. What is happening is so far beyond what we can know.

Lay your head under the tree of awe. Supernovas explode, lovers hold hands on garden paths, babies are born, bullets kill, Christ is crucified, birds glide in the light of dawn, our hearts break for all that is lost — there is no other response possible to the irreconcilable enormity of it all, but awe. The tree of awe isn't something that is finished. Its branches grow infinitely into the farthest heavens and into the most loving and agonizing moments of our lives. Lying here, looking up at it, there is nothing more we can say, but at least we know we are in good company.

The Face that Lights the Candle

GENEROUS IS A WORD THAT IS almost big enough to describe reality. After all, what could be more generous than this that allows everything to be everything? The hypothetical start of things — the Big Bang — that primal flaring forth was nothing if not Pure Generosity, no holding back — Here! A universe for you!

The nature of our sun is the same: its light given freely year after year, for billions of them! We live by the generosity of its light. Every glass of milk, every apple, every cup of coffee is given by its light, and we appear by the grace of that giving.

And what of this ever-unfurling spontaneous moment, how might we describe it but Purely Generous? Or this awareness that is the root of our being? We take our awareness for granted, we take the spontaneity of this moment for granted, and indeed they are just that: granted, given without our needing to ask.

This Vast Generosity we live within is free, unselfish, generative, unconditional — blessing us and everything with becoming. Its generosity is love itself. So if we need some guidance about how to live, this might be a good place to start — to contemplate the Ocean of Generosity we live in, and how every moment it makes its offering. There's no need to go out of our way to do this — every given breath reminds us!

You might say this view of an Ultimate Generosity as a guide for living is overly simple, and it is. There is more to the story —

The Pure Generosity of transparent light is met by opaque matter. Light goes every which way yet doesn't bump into itself. But matter, that other form of light, offers resistance. It absorbs and reflects. It waits in a form, and when it can sustain that form no longer it shape-shifts into another form. In each form it seeks to remain as long as possible. So now we have, in the midst of Universal Generosity: boundaries, self-definition, self-maintenance — that which does not give itself away like sunlight but seeks instead to maintain itself as itself.

Our lives are balanced right there — part of the Great Give-Away and yet charged to be these unique forms, for a time. Now the question of generosity as an ethic to live by has more depth. If you continually give away all the food on your plate, you'll starve. If you never give, you'll wither alone. How then shall we keep our balance between generosity and self-interest?

We see this question being played out in the politics of our time: for example, the desire to welcome refugees and the fear they will threaten us or weaken our identity. We see it in our personal relationships, when by always putting others' wishes before our own we risk losing our sovereignty. My sense of this question

— finding the balance between generosity and self-maintenance — is that in stating the question we've done most of the work. The act of holding the question reveals its answer. We find balance the way we do when we walk, by always being off-balance and then correcting. It's a good example of how non-duality shows up through duality: left foot, right foot, empty, full, giving, keeping, so the flowing flows without getting stuck at either pole.

But there's something else here, something this little contemplation on generosity and sovereignty might faintly point to. These words — generosity and sovereignty — are stubbornly *spatial*: sovereignty or self-maintenance is a concept that denotes a special place, a location where "I" am sovereign. In a parallel way, the word generosity denotes a transaction from "here" to "there," from giver to receiver. We conceive both of these ideas spatially. But that conception leaves us in a dualistic and fractional view of how things actually happen.

There's an enigmatic phrase from one of Rumi's poems: *"the face that lights the candle."* It makes us stop. *What? How could this be? Candles light faces, not the other way around.* But we're invited here to escape the linear logic of our language, just for a moment, and allow the generosity of the light and the uniqueness of the face to mutually arise, without one causing the other.

Mutually arise? How?

The apple ripening in the sunlight allows the sunlight to appear, to be sunlight. Without the apple, or any "thing" of matter, the sunlight would not be revealed. It would just go on and on, and never become visible. At the same time, as we know, the sun gives birth to the apple. No sun, no apple.

And so it is with our sovereignty: our being this unique being is made possible by our generous reciprocity with All Being. No generous reciprocity, no unique being. The Great Generosity itself makes possible what is sovereign, what is unique.

The candle lights the face, and the face lights the candle.

God Is Not Something Already Made

It can be humbling — and liberating — to recognize the limited nature of how we think. Our monkey minds swing from thought to thought, busily assembling our points of view. But when we look closely, we see that each thought is made out of words, and each word signifies a concept, and each concept — for example, the word and concept "God" — must remain static enough for us to "know" what is meant by it. If I tell you, "I believe in God," we both think we know what I mean. What is signified by the word "God" seems to sit somewhere for us both, like an object in space we can refer to even if we can't perceive it directly. By becoming an object in our sentences, God assumes the identity, in our minds and language, of something substantial in itself. "It" *exists* for us as an independent entity, already made.

This objectifying tendency of our minds — of how we think — is a necessary result of language. Each word we use *stands for* something that is not a word, and that "standing" presses our minds into the molds of objectification. This process is usually very helpful, as it allows us to communicate quickly and to navigate a world that, if it were perceived solely in its primordial unity, would not provide sufficient distinctions for us to survive. We, subjects, over here, perceive and communicate about those objects, over there, and we make our way among them. It's the powerful and helpful appearance of duality in what is, in its essential nature, nondual reality.

Henri Bergson, the great 19th/20th century French philosopher, continuously probes this objectifying tendency of our minds to help us recognize and free ourselves from its limitations. The phrase *God is not something already made* is his. "Something already made" is what we assume an object to be. An object *is* — we think of it as existing now as it was a moment ago and as it will be a moment from now. In the case of the physical objects around us, we now know through quantum physics that that is not how things are. Everything, even the hardest, seemingly most immutable diamond, is a humming mystery of quarks and energy potentials in constant flux.

But we would like our God to have a different status. We say, "He is now as He was and as He will be." But what are we referring to? What *is* this immutable quality of Godness? Is the idea of God's immutability a relic of our minds' objectifying tendencies? If so, is it possible for us to perceive or *know* Godness without objectifying "it"?

Bergson suggests we do have that capacity, although it is beyond the reach of our intellects. He calls this capacity *intuition*.

Our intellects, he says, can serve intuition, but only to a point —
then we need different wings. Bergson, who began his career as
a brilliant mathematician, uses many examples to help us take
flight. In one of them he recounts the old Greek philosopher
Zeno's story of Achilles' race with the tortoise, sometimes called
"Zeno's Paradox," which you probably heard about in school. In
the story, Achilles gives the tortoise a head start in the race, but
after that he can never overtake the tortoise, because in order to
do so he has to first cover half the distance between himself and
the tortoise, and then half the remaining distance, and then half
that, *ad infinitum*, so Achilles can never catch up. Zeno uses this
story to "prove" that movement is an illusion, and philosophers
and mathematicians have fussed with it ever since.

Bergson points out that a fundamental error is made in Zeno's
Paradox by transposing the notion of *time*, which is known by
movement (in this case Achilles' movement), onto *space*. Our
rational intellects, and the limits of Newtonian physics, reduce
movement and time into "things" that occupy successive "places"
in space, making them measurable, like the little lines on our
watches that mark minutes and seconds. Bergson contends that
this is where we get confused. Movement and time are not fundamentally transferable onto spatial places, although it is conve-
nient for us to do so for certain purposes. Instead, the nature of
movement and time is *flow,* and as flow, movement and time are
indivisible. We know that intuitively, though not rationally.

It's only natural that we humans would treat the idea of God in
this same way. To make God intelligible, our minds imagine God
as something that exists in space, something unchangeable and

"over there," already made. This habit of mind serves religions in that people can more readily conceive God as an *entity* to whom we can pray and whose commandments we should obey. But it is just this habit that has trivialized the enormity and mystery of Godness and turned many of us to the other extreme: rejecting the whole notion of Godness as an outmoded, superstitious concept. But when we do that, as is evident in much of contemporary secular society, we impoverish ourselves and risk losing the experience of the sacred in our lives.

We arrive now at the "payoff" of this philosophical inquiry, a payoff that has the potential to become wonderfully liberating, in an immediate, personal, non-abstract way. How so?

If God is not something already made, and if we accept that God is All, unbounded and omnipresent, then we — you and I — are not something already made either. Our moments, our thoughts, our most intimate experiences, are all *alive with becoming.* What we think is happening and what we believe to be true — even our most cherished beliefs, or our everyday opinions about the people in our lives, or our feelings about our own self-worth and our complaints about life — none of it is conclusive or inherently true. Nothing is already made. All is flow.

Reality, including this very moment for you and me and the whole enormous show everywhere, is inventing itself as it goes. It is alive and creative and free. Of course, each of those words, "alive," "creative," "free," can get stuck in our objectifying minds as things we think we *know,* but we have the intuitive capacity to let them loose, to sense them beyond their word-forms in the undefined, spontaneously creative openness that we share with

Godness itself. This is Bergson's famous élan vital, the living impulse that makes this endless, beginningless moment shine so brightly with becoming.

One with it — how could we be otherwise? — we are actually deathless: ever becoming, ever living, ever creative, ever free!

Children of Happiness

I WOKE BEFORE DAWN THIS MORNING and, seeing it was still dark, checked the clock. 5:10. Oh, I thought, I can sleep a little more. I curled back up under the covers and fell asleep for about ten minutes. During that time I had a dream, just one short, very clear scene: I was watching at a little distance what seemed to be a holy man talking with a few students. He had a shiny, perfectly bald head and he was smiling broadly as he spoke to them. I was struck by how the light sparkled off his bald head and the vitality he exuded as he spoke. I heard one sentence, but the words were very clear.

He said, *"Never forget, you are children of the vast beautiful happiness."*

Then I woke up, went to my study, and wrote down those words. When a dream has that kind of clarity for me, which is rare, and when I can hear the words spoken in it with precision, I pay attention.

What did the holy man mean by *"the vast beautiful happiness?"*

In what cosmos is that the reality? The picture of the universe given to us by science shows no evidence of a vast beautiful happiness. If anything, the universe is described as a vast cold vacuum with little spheres of nuclear fusion scattered here and there, stalked by black holes, everything speeding away from itself until, they think, no stars will be seen and one by one they will be snuffed out.

Scientific views of the universe cannot avoid being limited by the fact that they are derived from measurement and analysis. Scientists are loyal to empiricism, and bless them for that! But if we are to discover a more profound view of the cosmos, we need to use a different talent than measurement and analysis. The philosopher Henri Bergson suggests that this talent is *intuition*, which he describes as a simple and invisible experience of sympathy *"by which one is transported into the interior of an object in order to coincide with what is unique and consequently inexpressible within it."*

So to intuit the nature of the cosmos we must "coincide" with that nature. Since fundamentally we cannot help but be coincident with the universe, being transported into its interior would seem not just possible, but unavoidable. Yet that is not our experience. What gets in our way is our mental habit of objectifying what we perceive. Once we relax that tendency we can be "transported into" the nature or essence of all things.

The vast beautiful happiness that is the "interior" of the universe is not something that anyone can convince us of. Its realization must come first-hand. This is where the holy man's message that *we are its children* gives us some help. He's saying that we are the intimate *expression* of the vast beautiful happiness — from this happiness our own presence has blossomed. Now we know where to look. To intuit the universal happiness we need simply to open inwardly to what we are before any definition is applied. To the extent we can rest there, in ever-opening openness, the beautiful happiness becomes evident, without any evidence.

This is what the Tibetan hermit Shabkar Lama was pointing to when he said, *"When I remain in this state which is like a transparent, empty sky, I experience joy beyond words, thought, or expression."*

Back when I was a young seeker I remember being puzzled when I read these three words of the Indian Sufi, Inayat Khan: *"God is happy."* That sentence struck me as almost frivolous. Now I know what he meant. It's not the happiness we feel when things are going well, although that too is a small ray of it, a "child" of the parent happiness. The vast beautiful happiness is the great halleluiah of the whole thing, empty and radiant all at once.

For countless years, mystics have tried to reveal the great vast happiness with their words, knowing it was impossible, but I imagine at least it made them happy to try. Their trying has given us some hints, some reminders (*"Never forget!"* as the holy man said in my dream), a threshold of faith upon which our intuition can stand and swing open the door.

Here, to conclude, is a contemporary example of this kind of mystic reminder — Jack Kerouac's generous attempt to describe his experience of the vast beautiful happiness:

Pir Elias Amidon

It was the womb itself, aloneness, alaya vijnana
the universal store, the Great Free Treasure, the
Great Victory, infinite completion, the joyful
mysterious essence of Arrangement. It seemed
like one smiling smile, one adorable adoration,
one gracious and adorable charity, everlasting
safety, refreshing afternoon...

Mystic Nonsense

How strange it is we have forgotten where we came from and what we are. Immigrants from a place of light, we take our turns here building nests and finding food and soon we forget the Home we started from. This world makes us fear that place. We think there's nothing there, but we needn't worry. That place and this place are the same place, though they're not a place.

There is no place where the river's current is, no place where sunlight collects. There is only this Pouring Forth, and there is nothing from which, or into which, it pours.

It's not easy to talk about this, since it doesn't seem to make any sense. But it's helpful to have a feel for it because that feel can relax whatever fear we may have about dying, or living for that matter. After all, if a drop of water cried out it was afraid to flow over a rock, or rise up into a cloud, would that help anything?

The colors of this world are the colors of heaven, just from the inside out. Here we see the colors, there we are them. Here we play in God's Beauty, there we are that Beauty. Since here and there are fictions, everything's all right already. Free Medicine! Purifying, revivifying, sanctifying, we are the Holy Light we bathe in, we are the Good News we seek.

Pouring forth, neither you nor I have a moment to waste. Facing the firing squad, we smile and forgive. Even grief is a blessing. A solitary soldier comes to mop our blood and sees his reflection crying.

If a thousand Buddhas hovered in the air, you wouldn't see anything. All the dark oceans are empty light. After all, clear space doesn't part around us when we walk together, arm in arm by the river, confessing our love. But who are you, my love, who? Even you don't know.

The fountain flings its water-drops all night long, and inside each one, stars are twinkling. No one sees them, but in the morning, ducks swim under, taking a shower.

To follow the way that this doesn't make sense leads beyond sense-making to Presence-glimpsing, though without imagining a thing that is present. Our Enormous Home is not a place, though every place is Home. God is not a thing, though everything is God. God does not exist because God is not something already made. God is This. Like God, we too do not exist and are not something already made.

Because we imagine that we are something that *does* exist, we imagine we can die. We can't. That which does not exist cannot die. What we call *God* and what we call *us* is divine Delight, and where does Delight exist? No place. Just This!

Does that make sense?

Springtime Reverie

WALKING OUT YOUR DOOR ON A fine spring morning, the smells of the wet earth breathing into your body, for a moment without thinking, you feel the madness of spring *inside* you, you feel it coming up from the ground and moving through the air and moving right through you with its happy resurgence and it makes you want to sing, it makes you want to leave behind your little troubles and the world's big troubles and just be glad, and you are, for the moment, unreasonably glad and as fresh and as optimistic as it is, as if you were a child again blossoming out of time, carefree and giddy, and you wish you could skip or fly down the road or up with the flitting birds in the branches and it feels like you are indeed flying with them, your mind free from itself, free from being grownup and deliberate, and you want it to last, you want it to be this way forever because it feels so true, like a hint of a farther joy beyond even the springtime's delirium, a taste of that holy giving-ness that asks nothing for itself, the simple gladness of being, beyond meaning, beyond wanting, a whiff of that place without location, inside you, outside you, beautiful as the sky, as tender as your heart, realer than real, and you know it's true, but all of this lasts not longer than from here to there when again images from the morning's news come unbidden to your mind, the sharp flash you saw of a bomb in Ukraine, the face of distress on a mother huddled with her child, and you stop, caught between the spring's indifferent joy and the world's hurt, and you don't know what to do, or how to be, how to hold both the grinding injustice and the fragrant spring, the grief of your people and the happy freedom of your heart, and now you feel sorry for having felt so glad, so carefree just a moment ago, so in love with the spring, and you wonder, how can it be, how could God make springtime and devastation both in the same universe, how could it be that all is well and isn't at the same time, how could that impossible little question be answered that's plagued humanity ever since we started both praising the world and wanting to be free of its hurt, and you don't know an answer, and there, right under a blooming tree, knowing an explosion was ripping apart a home in Ukraine, you ask, you wonder, what can I do to ease the faraway pain and still not blame the spring for its gladness, you ask, you wonder, and then you do the only thing that's left to do, you raise your eyes and bless the spring and bless the hurt and turn away from neither.

Tears in Heaven

IN ONE OF HIS POEMS, KEATS wrote that the earth is "a valley where souls grow." In that valley we souls learn to love, and in that valley we learn that *everything and everyone we love comes to an end*. To love greatly, to dare to love greatly, we cannot escape the grief of endings. That is the way it is here.

Looking back at my life, I confess I have often resisted accepting this. Being of an optimistic nature, I thought our mortal life could be experienced either optimistically or pessimistically, either as a beautiful place of celebration or as a veil of tears, and when I was younger I just wanted the story to end with the words "and they lived happily ever after." But it doesn't work that way. The denouement (if there is a denouement) is not polarized like that. It took a long life for me to see there's another way to embrace the inherent dualism of our experience, the dualism of happy/sad, joy/grief, presence/absence, life/death.

Yes, the ultimate nature of the Real is, as the Tibetan Buddhists say, "All-Good," or as the Sufis say, it is "the perfection of love, harmony, and beauty." I am personally certain of this, not through thought or wishing, but in my bones. I know that sounds like a happy ending, and it is, and that our grief will be resolved in the All-Good, and it will, but not in the way we might think.

The words "the All-Good" and "the perfection of love, harmony, and beauty" are ways of trying to say the unsayable. They don't quite succeed because, while we think we know what they mean, meaning itself can't contain what the All-Good signifies. Whatever it is, and whatever we call it, the All-Pervading Presence of the All-Good encompasses time and all its productions, *and* the timeless, and is still beyond both time and the timeless. It encompasses all of space and everything that happens in space, and yet it is beyond all dimension. The All-Good absorbs into itself all our love and all our grief, like a majestic symphony. All of it matters.

"Jesus wept, though he knew the truth. Contemplating the world, enlightened Buddha shed a single tear." Our experience of earth life is not about arriving at a happy ending or a resolution to the pain and poignancy we experience here. Our journey is about the mystery of becoming and transfiguration. It is in this way that our grief, and our joy and love, are the valley in which our souls grow and are transfigured.

Time carves little lines in our faces, like canyons are carved into the earth's surface. Those lines and canyons are beautiful, and along with each white hair on our heads, they are hard won. By the time we come to die we are marked deeply by this life. The beauty we've experienced and the stupid mistakes we've made, the love we've shared and the losses we've endured, all of it comingles in our singular presence, in our *soul,* this most intimate crucible of transfiguration. "The soul is a current," Inayat Khan said, picturing our soul-crucible as a river, a flowing, an offering to the sea. In this image we may be able to glimpse how our love and grief are an inseparable whole, and how our tears make heaven glisten.

Love is the
Highest Ground

THIS WEEK IN AMERICA NINETEEN LITTLE children were shot dead in a classroom. The week before ten innocent people were gunned down in a grocery store. All the while Ukrainians and Russians were killing each other in muddy fields. We hear this, we know it's happening, and we don't know what to do.

These atrocities are in today's news, but they're not new. We humans are good at hurting and killing each other. It's estimated that during the An Lushan Rebellion in China (755-763 AD) 36 million people were killed. The Taiping Rebellion in China (1850-1864): 25 million. World War I (1914-1918): 24 million. World War II (1939-1945): 70 million.

Our minds blur at these statistics. How can we comprehend the violence and suffering within those abstract numbers? Nineteen children. 70 million men, women, children. Each one a tender life like ours.

Given some distance in time and space, victims and perpetrators blend into one immense tragedy. For whatever the reasons the An Lushan Rebellion was fought, those reasons fade in the stark reality of 36 million dead on all sides. The teenager who shot the little children this week was a victim as well as a perpetrator. That's not an excuse, it's just a fact. Every cruel act reveals how lost the perpetrator is. Tragedy encompasses all of it.

Seeing the enormity of the human tragedy like this — even getting just a glimpse of it — can drop us into numbness, or worse, into depression, nihilism, and misanthropy. Is there any other way to be present to the fearful meanness of our species? How can we hold all this interminable suffering?

We need to ask these questions — each one of us. *On what ground can we stand as members of the same human species that perpetrates so much hatred, and that suffers its unending consequences?*

To me, the answer is clear, though not at all easy to express. If we do not stand on the ground of love we will perish, personally and collectively. Love is the highest ground — groundless and grounded at the same time, beyond the dualities of good and bad and all the judgments that go with them, and yet present in the moment to the hard suffering of our people. It's the embrace of Jesus or the Buddha as they hold the world. It's unreasonable. It's love that doesn't depend on our earthly conclusions and verdicts.

Perhaps this great love is close to what the poet Galway Kinnell meant when he wrote, "the dream of all poems and the text of all loves" is "tenderness toward existence." That's the love that is called for as we behold, and try to hold, the tragedy of our species.

I remember years ago at a conference hearing Mother Teresa say in her frail voice, *"Love until it hurts."* That, too, may be a clue to answering these hard questions. The love that is called for is not comfortable, and it's not something we "do." It's bigger than us. I want to say it's divine, but that makes it sound distant, and it's not distant — it's real. As Trungpa Rinpoche remarked, "When tenderness tinged with sadness touches our heart, we know that we are in contact with reality."

I'm not sure this holy, painful, tender love will make things better, but that's not the point. The point is to not turn away, to *be* this love even as we witness its absence in the human world. As our species and the life of our whole planet face existential threats, may we find the grace to love like this — wider, deeper, unreasonably, until the end of our days.

The Benediction
of the Old Ones

In MID-LIFE I WOULD OFTEN WANDER through a beloved forest
a few miles from my home, a forest with no paths except for the
thin trails left by deer, and though it felt like I was wandering
aimlessly, I would typically find my way to one great tree towering up at the end of a ridge, and there I would sit with my back
against her, happy to be a small animal nestled against her trunk,
imagining myself to be one of her familiars.

I called her the "grandmother tree," and to be in her presence
was comforting to me, and steadying. I got in the habit of bowing
to her when I arrived at her grove. She was an old-growth hem-
lock, the only one of that age that I found in this forest, the rest
having been logged successively over the preceding centuries.
The loggers had probably spared her because she was at the end
of the ridge and difficult to get to, and because they hoped she

would seed new growth, or perhaps, like me, they simply felt awe in her presence. The grove she rose from felt hushed and sacred.

The human world I come from, on the other hand, esteems the new, the latest, the modern. To be young is to be desired. To be old is to be past one's prime. Usefulness and exuberance are honored, and old people are judged to have neither.

Now, having had the good fortune to arrive at the brink of old age myself, I'm beginning to sense there's something numinous possible at this end of life, a transmutation — while not guaranteed — from one's personal journey in life to something quite beyond the personal, something vaster and more meaningful.

When he was my age, the great writer Hermann Hesse spoke of this numinous possibility that is the province of the old:

> And the truth is, even if presumably in our younger years we have experienced more intensely and more dazzlingly the sight of a blossoming tree, a cloud formation, a thunderstorm, nevertheless for the experience that I'm referring to, one does need great age, one needs the infinite sum of things seen, lived through, thought, felt and suffered, a certain frailty and proximity to death in order to perceive, within a tiny revelation of nature, the God, the spirit, the mystery, the coming together of opposites, the great oneness. Of course, young people can experience this too, but less often, and without this unity of thought and feeling, of sensual and spiritual harmony, of stimulus and awareness.

Hesse is describing, in my view, the interiority of the elder — not the elderly, who may or may not be elders — but the unique capacity of the elder to hold the dream of life in its wholeness, simultaneously presencing the ages she or he has experienced, the grief and exultations, *"the infinite sum of things seen, lived through, thought, felt and suffered."* It's a rarefied state, bemused by the personal entanglements of our lives yet fully embracing them.

I feel this state, or "numinous possibility," is *an invitation to take our place among the old ones*, the ancestors, by whose commitment and sacrifices our species has survived, and we the living have been graced with life. It's a current that's trans-historical and trans-generational, a kind of spirit nourishment that gathers from the long generations of those who came before and streams through the millennia to us. Now it is our turn, those of us entering elderhood, to become part of that invisible stream of sustenance.

Taking our place with the old ones, becoming part of their sustaining power, is not a task we can apply ourselves to. It's not work. It's more like *a presencing* and *a bestowing*, like the grandmother tree was to me. She was old, the elder of the forest. There was dignity in her bearing, a quiet presence that was her gift.

Many old things — not only animate beings — carry this kind of dignity and blessing. Think of a mountain or a canyon. Think of a cathedral or an ancient stone circle. We go to these places and are touched by their "infinite sum of things seen," the weather they've endured, the passing of people worshipping, the seasons they've known. They too are elders to us, nourishing us.

And so it is with *the old ones* of our species — not only the elders still alive but all the elders of the past whose infinite sum of things seen flows through time like a benediction on us. We are invited — we who are proximate to death — we are invited to join this benediction. All that is asked is our whole-hearted presence and love.

You Bring Rivers

Rumi was referring to God when he wrote this line:

"You bring rivers from the mountain springs"

but couldn't the same be said of us? Do we not bring rivers of creative causation to this flowing moment, rivers arriving from countless sources? Our bodies, are they not rivers of genetic instructions, helixes, cell types, inherited traits informing how we live and respond moment to moment, informing our most intimate experiences? Are not our thoughts a current, our feelings a river? From what unseen springs do they come? Our very capacity to think and feel is a river of creative causation that made its way to us from our ancestors and the old ones before them, a river moving us now in our every inclination.

And the care we feel for each other, what is that but a current? Was our caring nature passed to us by the caring hands that coaxed us from the womb, or by the care of long generations of mothers and fathers, grandmothers and grandfathers, doing their best to assure warmth and sustenance for their young ones? How else did this caring nature come to us?

And these words we speak and hear and read, they come to mind so easily, yet the etymology of each one is a rivulet, a brook, a stream that flowed through countless lips, merging with others into the great river of our language that now we speak and hear so casually.

And what of the rivers of learning we've received, the guidance, the skills of speaking, the forming of words, the quiet study, the opening of our intelligence, the learning from mistakes we made, and the teachers, mentors, parents, siblings, friends, writers, artists, scientists, philosophers — each one a riverbank of the river they received and passed to us, all of it flowing and present in us now, a vast gift of guidance helping us on our way.

And with us too are the rivers of loneliness and hurt, despair, rivers of dying and the fear of dying, violence and woundedness, rivers of grieving, loss, all of it coursing through the generations and present in us now, creating, and birthing, our compassion.

Oh awesome rivers of time and rapids, slow meandering oxbows, quiet eddies, falls, rivers of causation and creativity flowing to us from the past, yet equally from the present, equally simultaneous, equally across time, connecting everything in at-once-ness, informing our present with all presents, even the future, whose becoming will be born of ours, whose river arrives from ours and informs our own even now, one river with all rivers, all at once, at once!

LOVE'S DRUM

When fear for the world is heavy upon us, or loneliness presses in, or we doubt ourselves and our power and purpose, let us remember the gift of the rivers we bring, the rivers that make us, the vast wild jubilant rivers we bring from the mountain springs.

The Other Side
of Death

LET'S TALK FOR A MOMENT ABOUT death. It's a dark and fearsome subject for many of us, especially at the time of this writing when we're all trying to hide from a fatal pandemic that's stalking the land, and every headline and news report counts the dead and reminds us we could be next. Death, usually in the background of our lives, is now in the foreground.

The desire to live, to avoid disease and death, is baked into our DNA — and it's a good thing it is. We mourn the death of those we love and do our best to save people we've never met from death. The cruel deaths of war are an abomination to us. It's understandable that death has a dark and fearsome reputation.

But what is it? What is death? Is it possible to understand it in another way, along with its dark reputation?

We may find some clues in the words of spiritual mentors, contemporary and past.

You probably know the story of the great Indian sage Ramana Maharshi, that when he was dying his disciples pleaded with him, "Master, please don't die! Don't leave us!"

Ramana replied, "Don't be silly, where could I go?"

Whenever I've repeated that story in a gathering, the reaction of nearly everyone has been an immediate smile or laugh. We get it. We get the joke.

What do we get? What do we know? After all, death is the big goodbye, the last farewell, the end of life.

Or is it? Why do we smile when we hear Ramana say he's not going anywhere?

When we look at death from the standpoint of our individual lives, it certainly looks like death makes people "go away," depart, vanish from life. But Ramana wasn't looking at death from the standpoint of his or our individual lives. Our particular lives do end; we have to accept that. Rather he was looking at it from the standpoint of our original, ever-present nature that doesn't go anywhere.

That may sound very spiritual, but what does it mean? What *is* our "original nature?" Is it alive? Is it not subject to death?

In Tibetan traditions, guidance is read aloud to those who are in the process of dying or who have just died, as in this verse of Padmasambhava:

Thine own awareness,
shining, void, and inseparable
from the Ground of Radiance,
hath no birth,

53

hath no death,
and is the Immutable Light.

As Ramana Maharshi testifies, we don't have to wait until death to recognize the Immutable Light that is our original nature. The essence of our awareness right now has *no birth, no death.* When we get a glimpse of this truth directly, an old tension that's been stretched tight in us relaxes and opens.

A profound gladness fills the human psyche
when it knows the part of the self that does not die.
> — *Coleman Barks*

And from Rumi:

We have such fear of what comes next. Death.
These loves are like pieces of cotton.
Throw them in the fire.

Death will be a meeting like that flaring up,
a presence you have always wanted to be with.

This presence is our original nature, present here and now, yet hidden from us because we're entranced with the phenomena that appear in it. The *profound gladness that fills our psyche* when we recognize what we are, comes from the realization that it's not simply "our" original nature but it's the original nature of everything, of the All, of the One. We can't fall out of it, even when we die.

Or as Thich Nhat Hanh says it:

> *Enlightenment for a wave is the moment the wave realizes it is water. At that moment, all fear of death disappears.*

And Rumi again:

> *Let sadness and your fears of death*
> *sit in the corner and sulk.*

> *The sky itself reels with love.*
> *There is one being inside all of us, one peace.*

Sufis often meditate on one of the Names of God called *Al Hayy*, the Alive. *Al Hayy* means that "God" — the pure awareness that is our original nature and the original nature of everything — is Alive. Rumi's *one being inside all of us* is Alive. It's an Aliveness not dependent on organic processes, and as such it is not subject to death. When our individual lives end, our original nature doesn't. As Sufi Inayat Khan told us, *"It is death that dies, not life."*

When you experience this directly (through spiritual practice or through a moment of grace) or if you simply accept it on faith, your attitude toward death changes. You still do everything you can to avoid death and you still grieve the loss of loved ones, but death is no longer dark or fearsome. It's a homecoming. You understand and can say with Walt Whitman:

> The smallest sprout shows there is really no death,
> And if ever there was it led forward life, and does not wait at the end to arrest it,
> And ceas'd the moment life appear'd.
>
> All goes onward and outward, nothing collapses,
> And to die is different from what any one supposed, and luckier.

The Beloved Community

IN THE EARLY 20ᵀᴴ CENTURY THE American philosopher Josiah Royce coined the term "the Beloved Community" as an ideal of social harmony brought into being by those loyal to goodness and truth. Later, the notion of the Beloved Community became central to the teachings of Martin Luther King Jr., who envisioned it as the ideal human community of love, solidarity, and justice that was "not yet" but that would eventually be actualized through our commitment to nonviolence and the sacredness of life.

It's a beautiful notion — *the Beloved Community* — stirring in us a sense of hope that humanity is indeed evolving toward a promised land. And it is just this *towardness* — "the arc of the moral universe is long, but it bends *toward* justice" — that inspires us, encourages us, and gives us the strength to believe we shall overcome some day no matter how bleak things look at the moment.

I say "amen" to that. We need hope, we need the faith in ethical progress that this vision offers us. But because it's a hoped-for ideal it can also feel a little abstract; because it's "not yet" — while the dysfunction of human societies is in our face — we can doubt that it ever will be.

I'd like to suggest that we might understand the notion of the Beloved Community as not only a beautiful future ideal toward which we are called, but that it's also a reality that's *here, now.*

The Beloved Community is all around us and within us. It's how our bodies function — the community of our organs and blood, nerves and bones, all functioning together in a wondrous wholeness. The air we're breathing, the water we drink, the food we ate at our last meal, are testaments to the Beloved Community we are part of. Everything is working together; everything is hand-in-hand.

The trees on the hillside draw sustenance from the earth through their roots, from the air and sun through their leaves. When their individual lives end, they give back to the soil and to the bugs and birds the richness their bodies have collected. The Beloved Community. When we walk on a path through a forest and feel calmed by the beauty of the dappled light, we are welcomed into the Beloved Community of beauty. When we say "thank you" to a stranger at the grocery store, those words rise up from our gratefulness for a small kindness, and — for a moment — the ideal society we hope for is made real.

From age to age, mothers have cuddled and sung to and

protected their babies. The Beloved Community. Every day the distant giant planet Saturn attracts stray asteroids that enter our solar system, shielding planet Earth from devastation. The Beloved Community. Scientists look for ways to produce clean energy, poets look for ways to express wonder, children laugh as they're carried on their father's shoulders. The Beloved Community. It's here, and at the same time, it's not yet.

When we perceive, even for a moment, how we are held in the community of life, how we are sustained within the vast web of all our relations, we gather strength to carry on and to serve the advent of the vision we dream of. Yes, the web of our relations can be torn — we see evidence of that every day — but with care it grows back.

Each act of kindness, selflessness, generosity, compassion, and communion heals and creates the Beloved Community. These acts, however inconsequential they may seem to us at the moment, are like seeds that contain within them our not-yet-realized goal. As theologian Paul Tillich describes it in the language of the Old and the New Testaments, *"the coming of the Kingdom of God* [the Beloved Community] *does not come in one dramatic event sometime in the future. It is coming here and now in every act of love, in every manifestation of truth, in every moment of joy, in every experience of the holy."*

Our ancestors, for all their failures and wars and missteps, longed for what we long for, and succeeded in bringing us to life and to this recognition of the better world we are capable of. We can draw strength from this gift of our ancestors — it's a strength that's here, now. The generations of humans to come

— our unknown descendants depending on us and cheering us on — we can draw strength from their encouragement too. It's a strength that's here for us, now.

Let us take heart in the Beloved Community, not only as a hopeful vision of the future, but as a vivid reality that arises "in every manifestation of truth, in every moment of joy, in every experience of the holy." It's both a reliable compass that will guide us through the dangerous times ahead, and it's here, now, our good home.

PRACTICES

The Joy of Pausing

THE AMERICAN CLOWN WAVY GRAVY ONCE famously said, "I come from the land of one thing after another." And so do we all! From getting out of bed in the morning to lying down tired at night, each routine and little task is followed by the next. Even when we take a break, those moments are quickly filled with distractions — chatting, thinking, reading, or watching a screen. One thing after another.

We can't avoid this — it's how the melody of life is played. This moment flows into the next, the current never stops. The problem for us comes when we feel pressured by the sense that too many things are demanding to be done next. That pressure is amplified when we worry about negative events we imagine could happen in the future. Then we feel compressed and tense, as if there isn't enough room for us in our own life. We lose our quiet center; we lose the sense that we are present and whole.

In my own life I've found that *pausing* helps when I lose my quiet center. By "pausing" I don't mean simply stopping what

I'm doing and sitting quietly somewhere, although that's always a good tonic. Pausing, as I experience it, can be done right in the middle of the river, and it can be as brief as a single breath. The length of a pause is not as important as its depth.

There are many styles of pausing — here are a few that work for me:

Pausing self-talk: Much of the pressure we feel in our life comes from the dominance of our mind stream, our self-talk. It's important to notice that self-talk has two partners: the one who's talking and the one who's listening. We explain things to ourselves as if there were two of us. To create a pause in the middle of self-talk, simply say to yourself, "Stop talking for ten seconds." You might be amazed to find how well it works! It may not last very long, but ten seconds is quite possible. In that pause, relax, take a breath, do nothing.

Pausing opinions: Opinions are points of view. They're less noticeable than self-talk since they supply the background flavors to our mind stream. Often we don't realize that we're pressured by our opinions; we simply assume they're the truth of what's happening. One way to notice our points of view is to recognize we're making judgments: "I have no time for myself;" "Nobody else is helping;" "It's always like this;" "My life is a mess." Once you spot that you're making a judgment, invite yourself to pause for a moment from its conclusion, from its certainty about being true. You don't have to argue with yourself about it, just allow for ten or fifteen seconds that it might not be true. In that pause, relax.

Pausing before you snap back: When we feel pressured by events, or people's demands on us, or when we feel misunderstood, it's easy to get irritable. Notice how irritability feels in your body, and when you feel that rise, pause before you say a word that will hurt, since it's like an arrow you can't call back.

Pausing when you wake: Pausing for a minute when you first open your eyes in the morning is a good and easy habit to cultivate. It's an intimate moment before anything is asked of you, a good time to feel thankful for your life, and to bless everyone and everything you can think of.

Pausing by asking: A humble question creates a pause. What's happening now? What am I doing? What am I feeling? The question doesn't presume an answer. It even lifts up its voice at the end — what's happening now? — and the mind sails off without a clue. There, for a moment, the mind is suspended in a healing pause.

Pausing in your heart: Typically we experience the center of our awareness as residing in our head, behind our eyes. For a minute or two, allow your awareness to drop down to the middle of your chest, to your heart center. Your heart is a wordless place, but it is caring and warm. Rest there. It may help to briefly recall images of people or aspects of life you care deeply about. Let yourself care from your heart and be grateful for what makes your life worth living.

Pausing in Nature's presence: We spend most of our time immersed in the culture and built environment of the human world, and feel we have little contact with free nature. Pausing in Nature's presence can remind us of our first belonging. Look at the sky; breathe in its spaciousness. Sit with your back against a tree and sense the life of its roots below and its branches above. Watch water flowing. Give yourself small moments where you feel how your animal nature is undivided from the living world. Pause there.

Pausing in timeless awareness: The Indian sage Nisargadatta once advised a student who asked for guidance, "Go back! Go back!" Go back to the place where you begin, right now, the place of spacious awareness that hosts all the phenomena you experience. It is a simple move, although nothing really moves. Just open up to the clearing you already are and pause there for a moment or two. When you do that your whole life is refreshed.

Quietness

SAY YOU WAKE UP ONE MORNING and notice that something is different about you. There's a beautiful quietness *inside* your body that you haven't felt before. It seems to emanate from the middle of your chest, a clear quietness opening from your heart area, filling the entire volume of your body. You sense how your skin envelopes this silence, but inwardly it seems to be without limit. The quietness disappears into the depths of your body without coming to a boundary.

It's an unfamiliar feeling but not alarming; it has a peaceful and spacious quality to it. So you sit in a chair and allow the inward quietness to have its way with you. You notice that you can't really stand outside of the quietness to look at it — it takes up the whole interior of your body. There's no place for you to be except within the quietness and pervaded by it.

Your attention is drawn to the boundary of the quiet where it touches the inside of your skin. You feel how this inner silence defines the shape of your body. And then an extraordinary thing happens. The quietness within you seems to open right through your skin and expand outwardly, or perhaps it's just the opposite: the quietness of space outside your body instantaneously meets the quietness you feel inside. You are within the quietness and simultaneously held by it. Encompassed.

Although it's purely intimate with you, you sense the quietness also has a numinous feel of *otherness* to it. You *are* it while at the same time it's infinitely beyond you. Your private experience as a sensate body and distinct person arises within it and is somehow an expression of its vast, silent, and indefinable presence.

As you sit there experiencing all this, you feel a great tenderness — the quiet that pervades you and encompasses you is alive with a kind of tender warmth, though not a warmth of temperature. It's intimate and tender and not even approachable by these words. You feel safe.

After some time you get up from your chair and begin to attend to the necessities of the morning. At first the presence of the boundless, intimate, and safe quiet is still palpable to you — it's everywhere as you move around and as normal sounds and sensations occur. Its intimacy unites with the phenomena of the world around you — you are within everything while at the same time you remain your unique bodily experience.

The sense of tenderness pervades your awareness of the people and things you encounter. When you touch something, a button on your shirt, a piece of toast, a cup of coffee, your touch seems to come from the tender quiet you have recognized. When you listen to someone speaking, and when you speak, the words seem to come from and be held by the same tender quiet. The sense of safety makes you gentle and unhurried.

Later, when you realize the world's noises and your own thoughts and feelings have obscured the all-pervading quiet, you start to feel annoyed with yourself and with the people around you for taking the quietness away.

That's when a second extraordinary thing happens. As you notice your annoyance, you see it for what it is. You see it's given you a position from which to complain. The moment you feel the constraint of that position, you experience yourself outside it, as if you no longer needed to care whether the quiet has been obscured or not. You relax. The feeling that you're missing something falls away, and in that instant, glory be, the tender quietness opens from your heart again as if it never left.

Gentleness

IF WE'RE LUCKY, AT SOME POINT in our life's spiritual journey we may hear the news that the realization we've been seeking is already here in this moment.

Where? How?

We're told: *Just relax. Open. Stop doing anything. Stop searching for anything. Simply be the presence of now.*

Guidance like this can be helpful, but it can also feel abrupt and bewildering. How do I relax in such a radical way? I can tell myself to relax and to open, but by what signs will I know the way? To simply be the presence of now without doing anything or searching for anything sets me adrift. What will help?

We can find a hint in response to these questions in the work of the 3rd century Greek mystic, Plotinus. Plotinus often called God by the name *"the Good"* and recognized that the numinous reality of the Good is all-pervading and ever-present. Here he gives us his hint:

"The Good is gentle…and is always at the disposition of whomever desires it."

Let's hear that again: *the gentleness of the Good is always at the disposition of whomever desires it.* Pierre Hadot, the great French historian, describes it this way:

"Plotinus' entire life consisted in the experience that gentleness, like grace, proclaims the presence of the Principle of all things."

The guidance here is that we can learn how to relax, how to open into openness, and how to simply *be* the presence of now, by following the scent of gentleness. Gentleness is the sign and the assurance, and we can feel this "gentleness" spontaneously and directly in our body.

Try it. Next time you sit in meditation, doing your best to relax and to open, follow the gentleness. You'll know it by its welcome. *"There is a sun warmth inside, nurturing the fruit of your being,"* Rumi tells us, *"…a love-breath that lets you open infinitely."* Let its gentleness pervade your mind and heart and body. It's already present so you don't have to make it up.

If you feel stuck in old patterns of self-identity or nervousness, you can start by noticing the gentleness of your breath, especially how gently each breath appears and disappears so subtly. Let it assure you.

Gradually the gentleness of your very presence will reveal itself. Let that gentleness take you. Whatever stories, fears, or grief might trouble your daily life, whatever pains or depressions you may feel, give them to the gentleness.

The gentleness of the Good is not a thing. It's more like a fragrance, a familiar love, a warmth, acceptance, safety. It's completely kind. It's why Sufis call it "the Friend."

You might ask, "The Good, the Friend, this gentleness — do I have to *believe* in all this?"

I think it helps, at least to begin with. If you don't naturally feel what this "gentleness" is, start by pretending you feel it. After a while it will be evident. Then believing won't be necessary.

Toward the end of his life, Plotinus became increasingly aware of the importance of learning how to live our day-to-day life guided by our contemplation of "the gentleness of the Good." As long as we're embodied in this human form, he saw that our task is to bridge our experience of the purity of the Good with our experience of daily life. Gentleness is that bridge.

When we notice, for example, that we're being judgmental, irritable, or out of rhythm, what happens? Through the very gentleness of our noticing, our irritability and self-preoccupation subside. We apologize. We become simpler, gentler.

Following the gentleness of the Good is indeed a simple and ancient ethic. The Vedas said it: *Let all the world be my friend!* Jesus said it: *Love one another.* The Dalai Lama said it: *My religion is kindness.* The Quran said it: *"The servants of the Merciful One are those who walk gently upon the earth."*

In the turmoil of our times, learning to walk gently upon the earth, following the gentleness of the Good — by its grace we will find our way forward.

Selflessness

No matter what spiritual path you take — Sufi, Buddhist, Christian, Jewish, Muslim, Taoist, Advaita, Dzogchen — one day you arrive at a sheer cliff where the path ends.

At that precipice you face a seeming void: *the voiding of your self.* It can be a scary place, and most of us have had the experience of turning around at that point and making camp back in the familiar hills of our specific path, to be assured by its practices, stories, and promises. After all, who in their right mind would step off that cliff? There must be another way around! If I want awakening, enlightenment, freedom — if I want to be in God's presence — I want to be there when it happens, and not voided in some spacey emptiness.

It's not surprising there is confusion about this. *Selflessness, ego-death, egolessness, fana* (the Sufi term), *psychic death* (the Jungian term), *self-transcendence, self-surrender, the dark night of the soul* — however it's been described — the precipice and what it represents feels like a threat to our sense of rootedness as existent beings. It seems only natural to withdraw from its edge.

Since birth we've struggled to establish our moorings in this reality by identifying our "self" with various layers of our experience, whether it be our body, our gender, ethnicity, religion, opinions, or other more subtle forms of identification. Of course, there's some utility to this, at least when we can hold our self-identifications lightly. But when we hold them *tightly*, when we assume that what we identify ourselves with represents the truth of what we are, we set ourselves up for conflict and suffering.

We may have heard this expressed a thousand times in the teachings of our spiritual path, and we may accept it intellectually, but the obliteration we fear as we waver on the precipice of selflessness can still make us pull back from opening into its spaciousness.

There's a simple way to practice relaxing our grip on our self-sense that's available to us at every moment — if we can recognize it for what it is. We don't have to be in a refined state of meditation or self-analysis; it's an opening offered to us continuously and it doesn't take any preparation to experience it. *Simply be present, right now.* It's easy because it's already given to us. There's nothing we have to do to make it happen.

Notice that when you turn your attention to the presence of this very moment, there's a little gap. It may only last for a few seconds. It's when you relax from doing anything at all, when you stop reading these words, when you're in-between thoughts and you're not busy judging what just happened, or planning what might happen next.

Notice that in this gap there's no sense of "you." Your memories are not there, your language is not there, your attitudes about things are not there. Of course, you could bring up a memory, or a word in your language, or an attitude you have, but in the simple presence of this moment, none of that is present. Even your name is absent, even your gender, even your religion — there's just this empty, open, clear moment, and it's selfless.

Learning to relax knowingly in this present moment, even for periods of a few seconds, purifies us. It's like when we were kids on a hot summer day in the back seat of the car, rolling down the window and letting the wind blow against our face. Eyes closed, smiling.

It doesn't take being an advanced practitioner to let this happen. It's not even scary, since this gap is familiar and doesn't carry the big name of "ego-death" with it. For a moment or two, you know yourself without your identities and attitudes — you're just here, without being "you." Empty and fresh and present.

These little moments of purification are available to us at any time, and the more we refresh ourselves in them the easier it is for us to realize that selflessness is not something frightening or obliterating. It's our natural state, and we've known it all along.

The Place Where
Nothing and
Everything Meet

IF YOU WALK INTO A FOREST and put your ear against a tree, you will hear a silence in there that is like your own. It is a silence that has no end. Empty silence is the background to everything we perceive, in the same way that space is the background to everything we perceive. Most people don't like listening to that silence because it makes them feel alone, and they equate aloneness with loneliness. But the silent aloneness inside us — and inside all being — is not lonely.

The Zen master Katagiri Roshi once said, "When you see the bottom of your life, you see emptiness right there. You are standing by yourself, completely left alone in emptiness. That is a very deep sense of aloneness."

Accepting emptiness like this, accepting our perfect aloneness, is not isolating; it is an essential part of our awakening. As Katagiri puts it, accepting emptiness allows us "to stand up in a new way." When we stand up like that, with recognition of the ground of emptiness everywhere, we enter the reality of what he calls *togetherness and creativity.*

By accepting our perfect aloneness we embrace our perfect togetherness. Our aloneness extends to others because we see that everyone shares this same empty nature. "A bodhisattva," Katagiri concludes, "constantly becomes alive from emptiness, and that life helps others."

Sufis have a different way to describe all this, but it amounts to the same thing. "Essence is emptiness," Rumi tells us. "Emptiness brings peace to your loving." And this:

> *Dear soul, if you were not friends*
> *with the vast nothing inside,*
> *why would you always be casting your net*
> *into it, and waiting so patiently?*
> *This invisible ocean has given you such abundance…*

And this:

> *…lying in a zero circle, mute…*
> *when we have totally surrendered to that beauty,*
> *we will have become a mighty kindness.*

The Sufic equation of dissolving into emptiness and emerging as love is identical with the image of the bodhisattva constantly becoming alive from emptiness. It is the movement of awakening described in Sufi teachings as *fana* and *baqa*. *Fana* is deconstruction of the self-illusion, most often translated as annihilation of the self. "I honor those," Rumi says, "who empty the self and have only clear being there."

Baqa is what comes after. As Coleman Barks describes it: "*Baqa* is the coming back from annihilation with cleansed enthusiasm for particulars. In the state of *baqa* one reenters the moment fully, doing small quiet work, sewing the robe of absence." This is "standing up in a new way," the way of togetherness and creativity. Or, as Sufis might say, it is the expression of *love* and of *doing the beautiful* that naturally flows from emptying oneself into clear being.

In my own life this "move" has become a practice that happens — in shortened form — dozens of times each day. Let's try it together now. As you follow the practice below, notice the subtle kinesthetic sensations that occur in you. When you do this a number of times, those sensations will begin to elide, and the "practice" will happen almost instantaneously.

As you sit reading this, notice the clarity of your vision. Notice there's nothing in the way of your seeing these words.

Now notice the clarity of the awareness in which these words appear. That clarity is unobstructed — there's nothing in the way of the words appearing in your awareness; there's no color or background, your awareness is perfectly clear.

Bring your attention now to the space between your

forehead and the back of your head. Notice that the space inside your head is also perfectly clear. This clarity is emptiness.

Notice the sensations of your breathing. Notice how each inhale arises out of nothing and, at the top of your in-breath, it vanishes into nothing. Your out-breath does the same. Very gently, notice the space surrounding and pervading each breath. Recognize its clear, empty quality.

Now allow your intuitive openness to expand, seeing how this clarity, this empty quality, is not bounded by anything — it is all around and through you, it is everywhere, like space is everywhere.

There is nothing you need to do to "hold" this recognition of the empty quality that pervades you and all the people and phenomena you encounter; it is always present. Relax in, and as, this clear, empty presence.

This is the "intentional" aspect of this practice. What happens next is where the magic is — *baqa*, "standing up in a new way" — re-entering the moment with "cleansed enthusiasm for particulars." However this occurs will be unique to you and the moment you are part of.

The place where you stand up is the place where nothing and everything meet. It's not a place where your intellect will be of much use. We might call it a "heart space," though it's a heart space that pervades reality, not just the space inside your chest. In the place where nothing and everything meet, love opens all by itself, amazed and kind and creative.

Pir Elias Amidon

Only this ancient love
circling the holy black stone of nothing,
where the lover is the love,
the horizon and everything in it.

— *Rumi*

Living in the
Zero-Point-Now

I WANT TO TALK HERE ABOUT *living in the zero-point-now* and
what the future and the past have to do with that, and right off I
should warn you that I'm going to try to do this by using the narrative voice of a 17-year-old boy named Herman who's the main
character in a novel I'm reading, since his voice isn't concerned
with run-on sentences and he free-associates better than I do. If
you get confused about who's talking, me or Herman, just imagine it's Herman, even though you know it's me. Actually I was a
17-year-old boy once, so it's not such a stretch.

The thing I especially like about Herman is that his voice just
hums along like this, and even when he doubts himself he does it
in the same humming-along way and doesn't seem to care what
anyone thinks, even if he says he does. Speaking of humming
along, and to turn to our subject, isn't that what the future does?
I mean, here we all are in the zero-point-now, and instantly it

turns into something else and keeps humming along, and yet all the while it stays the same: the zero-point. So how does "now" know what to do next? And where does "next" come from?

I used to think I was in charge of what comes next, or at least what *should* come next, and I'd get in a tangle talking to myself about what I liked and didn't like and how things should be changed, and then I'd walk around being the person who had that attitude. I still do that more often than I care to admit, but I want to tell you I've found a fast way out of the tangle, and it's easier than it sounds.

The zero-point-now.

That's it. I just say those words and they remind me to drop everything I'm talking to myself about and everything I'm complaining about or wishing was different, and I just step into the zero-point-now, which isn't hard to find since it's always where I left it. It's right here where everything that's about to happen starts, and when I'm here "in" the zero-point-now I don't know what's going to happen next but that's perfectly fine. It's like not knowing where the ping-pong ball is going to bounce on the table but playing it as best you can, which means letting the zero-point play it.

If I start talking to myself again and having an attitude about how things should be, the zero-point-now vanishes almost immediately and I fall back to being a person with an attitude and I get caught again in the tangle. But the good thing is, it doesn't seem to matter how often this happens since the zero-point-now is always here to untangle things if I just remember what's happening and say "zero-point-now," and step into it. Well, it isn't really "stepping" because I don't actually move anywhere, but I think you know what I mean.

I once asked a writer friend of mine how he came up with what happens next in all the stories he writes. He told me, just imagine that you're at the theater and a play is about to start. The house lights go dark, the curtain rises, a man in a scruffy suit enters stage right, looks over his shoulder and then says... Listen to what he says, my friend told me. Write it down and keep going — which I take to mean don't try to make it up yourself, just be part of its appearing. The curtain rises, something happens, but there's no need to claim it's you dreaming it up. I can't even claim it's me who's dreaming up the next words in this sentence — they just appear no matter how much I think it's me doing it.

So where does what's about to happen come from? The past? Does the past *make* the future? It certainly has something to do with it, otherwise there wouldn't be any words to come next in this sentence. All these words are just echoes of earlier words, all the way back to when they were nothing but the grunts and coos of some old girls sitting around a fire cooking a rabbit in a long-ago forest. Now that I think of it, this pencil in my hand was made in the past by someone who's doing something else now, and this chair I'm sitting on, and the cloth of my shirt. I have no idea who stitched my shirt together, this piece to this piece. It happened in the past, in someone else's zero-point, but here it still is, wrapping around me in my own zero-point-now. That's wild. All the zero-point-nows that have ever happened — the zero-points of the making of my shirt and the dreaming of the words and everything else — are a part of *this* zero-point-now!

Still, even though that's true, it's not the whole story. Something else is happening that isn't just cause and effect — the past isn't just pumping out the future. But however it works, it's not something I can figure out and tell you about. It's something magical. Spontaneous. All you can do is step into your zero-point-now and be part of its spontaneity and feel it for yourself. You'll feel that *everything that happens, spontaneously changes,* while at the same time *the zero-point-now spontaneously happens without changing,* which is a way of saying the zero-point-now happens without happening.

One last thing — and maybe this is the most helpful thing about all this: *the more I get to being in the zero-point-now, the more I seem to disappear.* Try it yourself. It's not scary, like being obliterated, but something for sure disappears. I step into the zero-point-now and poof! no more me with an attitude!

And then? All I can say is — *I get happy!* Everything seems fresh and clear as a bell. I feel free, wide open, at ease and ready for the ping-pong ball wherever it comes from. I can't say for certain this will happen for you, but it might. Anyway, that's what I have to say about living in the zero-point-now, and what the future and the past have to do with it.

True Illusion

My little cat jumps into my lap as I start to write. I sit back to give her space. She curls in a spiral like a nautilus shell, closes her eyes, and sleeps. She doesn't know what is happening. She hasn't been following the news.

Her ears flick slightly. I think she's dreaming. Whatever she's dreaming about seems real to her, at least until she wakes up. Then another "reality" will appear to her which she'll accept as real. To me, both her dream-reality and her waking-reality — if I could experience them — would likely seem partial, limited, not the "true" depiction of the world that I have. They would seem to me dream-like — brightly apparent, yes, but fictive, not really existing in the way they seem to exist to her.

But what's to say that's not also true about my own waking-reality? I know the dream I had last night was not real, at least I do now, but what about this waking-reality? Could it also be dream-like — a fictive illusion created by my own limited interpretation of what's happening, just the same as my cat's limited interpretation of what's happening?

How do we tell what is real? We measure the space between things, we knock on wood, we stroke the cat, we count the time between one event and the next, and by all this evidence we become confident there is a real world *out there* that exists as we perceive it. My lap, the cat, my neighbor's garage, the sun climbing into the morning, all *truly* existing.

But then, what do we make of these lines from Rumi:

> *Out of unconditional emptiness comes this planet with all its qualities.*

Is *this* true? If it is, if "this planet with all its qualities" comes out of unconditional emptiness, it must be doing that right now, not just in the primordial past. This moment with all its attendant perceptions spontaneously appears, but how? From where? And doesn't it instantly vanish, right now, back into "unconditional emptiness? In the infinitely short duration of the present instant, *can any of this that is appearing really claim "existence"?* Perhaps what we assume to be reality actually *is* a kind of dream, a mirage, an evanescence no more substantial than the play of light on the surface of a pond, or the changing shapes in a mirror.

This radical form of inquiry and contemplation is at the heart of the Dzogchen tradition of Tibetan Buddhism. While present in early Buddhist sutras and the teachings of the 2nd century Nagarjuna, it was precisely described as a practice by the 14th century master Longchenpa in his famous manual *Finding Comfort and Ease in Enchantment.* (There are several translations of this text available; Keith Dowman's translation entitled *Maya Yoga* is, in my view, the most accessible, poetic, and illuminating.)

Longchenpa's text gathers eight analogies to help describe our ephemeral experience of reality: it is like a dream, like a magical show, like an optical illusion, a mirage, the reflection of the moon on water, an echo, a magic city, an apparition. With each analogy he prescribes the same basic practice: that we apprehend all our experience as *maya*, illusion, mirage, a magic show, etc. Here he describes the dream practice:

> *The outer world, its mountains and valleys, villages and towns and its living beings, compounds of earth, water, fire, air and space, all forms, sounds, smells, tastes and sensations, the five sensory objects, and the internal world of body-mind and its sensory consciousness, all experience, should be attended to incessantly as dream.*

It's not surprising that our minds rebel at this suggestion. We're not ready to concede that the world of phenomena around us — and that we're part of — is a dream. Surely not! This great heavy earth, the oceans, the mountains...

And then once more, Rumi drops this on us:

> *The here-and-now mountain is a tiny piece of a piece of straw blown off into emptiness.*

If this is true of the mountain, what about all the suffering in the world, the wars, the bombs slamming into buildings — are these also a dream, blown off into emptiness? And the people we love, our children and grandchildren, the work we do, everything we hold dear — are these a dream? Doesn't this practice of apprehending all experience as dream diminish the value, depth, and joy of life?

Here I can only say, try it. Try attending to all your experience as dream, at least for short bursts. See what happens. In my experience the value, depth, and joy of life is *not* diminished by this practice, in fact just the opposite. But descriptive words here about "what happens" when you attempt this practice are not very helpful. Just try it yourself and see.

This *maya yoga* — attending to all experience as *maya* — is known as one of the most direct "short-cuts" in Dzogchen. In attempting it, you may sense for a brief moment something of what Longchenpa calls a state of "empty clarity" that shimmers "with an unbroken natural happiness." Curiously, in that empty clarity the world doesn't go away just because it's seen as evanescent. After all, in a lucid dream when we're sleeping — when we wake *in* the dream and know it's a dream — the dream-world doesn't disappear. We remain in its "enchantment," but we're no longer bewitched by it. We're at ease, as in Longchenpa's title: *finding comfort and ease in enchantment.*

Peter Fenner, the Buddhist nondual teacher, once remarked that an illusion is illusory only as long as we are fooled into believing it is real. When we recognize our perception of reality is an illusion it ceases being an illusion! It becomes what I call *true illusion,* and the comfort and ease that ensues has a playful quality to it: we are unattached to the dream but intimately and compassionately responsive with it, "at play in the fields of the Lord." Or as Keith Dowman writes, "To regard every situation as a magic show is simply to relax and enjoy it."

Of course, our capacity to do this is weak; we've spent our entire lives asserting that the phenomenal world is real, not a dream or a magic show. Now and then we may get an intuition of this comfort and ease, but the density of apparent reality quickly reconstitutes itself. Remember what the old Taoist sage Chuang Tzu said:

> *Only after the great awakening will we realize that this is a great dream. And yet fools think they are awake, presuming to know that they are rulers or herdsmen. How dense!*

So you and I, writing and reading this together, what are we? How can we understand this? Are we real? Are we a dream? What are we?

Let's give Rumi the last word:

> *We are the night ocean filled with glints of light. We are the space between the fish and the moon, while we sit here together.*

The World's Mirror

THERE'S A ZEN STORY THAT GOES like this: A donkey wanders over to a well in a courtyard and looks into it. What he sees is a donkey down there looking up at him. At the same time, so the story goes, the water in the well looks up at the donkey and sees itself reflected in the donkey's eyes — it sees water. What is seeing what?

Of course, it's a silly story — we know the donkey is the donkey and the water is the water, and yet what's pointed to in the story is a crack in that arrangement where something else can be glimpsed. Something else?

If you were to imagine for a moment that the world you're experiencing is a mirror — like the water in the well — it's possible that you'll get a hit of a sensation that feels something like *transparency*. First you imagine that the world "out there" is your reflection — that what you are seeing and feeling in the moment is actually reflecting what you are. And then curiously enough, you may be visited with a sense that you are neither this nor that — that you are transparent.

Try it for a moment: look away from this page and imagine that what you are seeing and feeling is your reflection looking at you. *Include not only the visual field you're perceiving but your whole emotive and ever-changing experience that comes with this moment.* No need to think about it, just let what you see and feel in the moment represent a vivid reflection of what "you look like." Do that several times. Now close your eyes and imagine that the sensations you're aware of — your breathing, your body sensations, the sounds you hear, the thoughts that come by, and *"your whole emotive and ever-changing experience that comes with this moment"* — imagine that all this is your reflection looking back at you.

If you can manage this, you may receive a sense that the "you" you consider yourself to be loses its privileged position. You may feel yourself both as the immediate world of your experience, and simultaneously *not* that. You may have the equally curious sensation that the properties of the world you are perceiving — for a moment at least — lose their "thatness." You sense they're not other than you... and since you are transparent, they are too.

Rumi's poetry is filled with reports of this same experience — here are a few examples:

> *We are wisdom and healing,*
> *roasted meat and the star Canopus.*
> *We are ground and the spilled wine sinking in...*

We look like this, but this is a tree,
and we are morning wind in the leaves
that makes the branches move.

Silence turning now into this, now that.

∼

You're sitting here with us, but you're also out walking
in a field at dawn. You are yourself
the animal we hunt when you come with us on the hunt.
You're in your body like a plant is solid in the ground,
yet you're wind.

∼

The raucous parrots laugh,
and we laugh inside their laughter,
the two of us on a bench in Konya,
yet amazingly in Khorasan and Iraq as well.
Friends abiding this form,
yet also in another, outside of time, you and I.

∼

The whole of existence is a mirror whose essence you are.

We know that the essence of a mirror is transparent. It doesn't show up as anything in itself, yet in it everything shows up. In the same way, we are the world's mirror, and as we have just glimpsed, the world is our mirror. When we look into the world's mirror even for a moment, we see that the world is us and we are the world. This glimpse reveals how everything is intimate and happening together, and how you and I and the whole world, all its beauty and all its ugliness, are one body.

Looking in the world's mirror opens our heart's door. Dare we leave it open? We might think we would be overwhelmed by such vulnerability, but to the extent we experience ourselves as transparent, there's nothing in the way that can be overwhelmed. We can simply be present and responsive in whatever way is appropriate. We can be, as Rumi says, "the jar that pours."

> *We are the mirror as well as the face in it.*
> *We are tasting the taste this minute*
> *of eternity. We are pain*
> *and what cures pain, both. We are*
> *the sweet cold water and the jar that pours.*

Good Work

THERE'S A LOT OF HARD TALK these days about societal collapse. People are getting scared. Young people are seriously wor-
ried about what the future holds. There's the specter of climate
change, pandemics, economic breakdown, species extinction, air
pollution, soil depletion, the scarcity of clean water, increasing
racism, xenophobia, refugees, the proliferation of arms, despotic
governments, systemic injustice, overpopulation — the list goes
on and on.

It feels distasteful to me to recite it again — you already know
all of this — why spend your precious time reading about it again
when there's not much you can do about any of it?

This sense of hopelessness and disempowerment is what I
want to speak to here — the feeling that we can make no substantial change in this juggernaut of social and ecological collapse. I
believe we *can* contribute to real change, and that we do, every
time we turn our hearts, minds, and bodies to what I'm calling
here *good work*.

What's good work? Any work that heals. Any work that protects and nurtures life in its wholeness. Any work that contributes to the beauty and flourishing of the community of life on earth. It's that simple.

The challenging practice for each of us is to ask of whatever work we find ourselves doing: "Is this good work? Does it heal? Does it protect and nurture life? Does it contribute to the beauty and flourishing of life on earth?"

We must ask it of our careers. We must ask it of the work our company or institution is engaged in. Does this work nurture life? Does it contribute to life's beauty and to the possibility of joy and communion? These are demanding questions; they quickly reveal how much of what we humans do diminishes life rather than nourishes it.

I realize this may sound simplistic and even naïve, especially when whole books could be written about what I'm trying to express in a few hundred words. We know the vast economic system we're part of is enormously complex and all-encompassing, dedicated as it is to resource extraction, growth, consumerism, and militarism, with profits going to the rich and powerful. It's easy to feel caught inside this remorseless, churning machine, and even if the work we're doing isn't good work, we can feel that we simply have no choice. We need the job. We need to provide for ourselves and our family. When that's the case, of course, do what's necessary, but don't stop there. Make it your life's intention to find good work. Keep looking. Get creative. As soon as it's possible to do so, abandon whatever life-defeating work you're doing and find work that serves life. If you're a young person just starting out, dedicate your talents to finding and creating good work, work that helps build a better world. No matter how small your gesture may seem, it's the only difference that will make a difference.

And one more thing, now that I'm giving advice: even good work can become anti-life if we treat it as drudgery. Sweeping the floor, chopping vegetables, washing the windows — these tasks definitely nurture life, but that nurturing can be betrayed by our attitude if we resent doing them. The other day I was trying to fix a small leak in the plumbing in the crawlspace under our house, a task I felt fine doing, until I had to wriggle under a pipe on my belly through the dust and cobwebs, and suddenly I cursed, feeling irritated and sorry for myself. The sound of my curse stopped me. I lay there in the dust and realized what I was doing — I was making good work into bad work. I was letting a challenging situation for my aging body infect my spirit with annoyance and self-pity. That's all I needed in that moment, that realization. My irritation vanished. I kept wriggling along, got to where I needed to be, and fixed what needed fixing. Good work, all of it.

The point I'm hoping to make here is that in the face of all that's going wrong, all that's mean and destructive and unholy, neither complaining nor giving up will change the trajectory we're on. Our very best chance of making a better world is for each of us to find and create good work, the work that needs to be done. There's so much of it!

Befriending Unfriendliness

WHILE THE WORLD WE ENCOUNTER DAY to day is not always friendly, it is our job to befriend it. Of course, befriending the world's unfriendliness is a profound challenge; it requires equanimity and a great capacity for love and compassion. When Jesus was being nailed to the cross he prayed that his executioners be forgiven. Although we may honor his response as an ideal, when someone criticizes us or expresses animosity toward us, what is our response? Most often we react with defensiveness: we try either to defend ourselves or to return the attack in ways that will diminish the accuser. Yet we can see from the world's history of conflict, violence, and revenge the predictable outcomes of this kind of reactivity, just as the many small examples we can think of from our own lives show us the painful results of our own defensiveness.

Befriending unfriendliness is not something easy to accept, especially when we consider the horrendous examples of victimization and oppression throughout human history — befriending that unfriendliness can look like passivity, cowardice, or betrayal. As a conscientious objector during the Vietnam War, I grappled at length with the dilemma of pacifism — and it is far beyond the scope of this essay to deal with its many nuances — but most succinctly, for me it comes down to "situational ethics": our job is to befriend the world, yes, but sometimes so many mistakes have been made, so many opportunities for befriending have been missed, that there is no alternative but to say *No!* and to stand up to oppression, as the Allies did when they stood up to the Nazi war machine in the Second World War. Befriending must be our natural response in nearly every situation we encounter, but when it is too late and the only recourse to prevent even greater disaster is through force, then the use of force may be justified.

But then what? This is the crucial point — there are endless possibilities for the healing power of friendship to avert violence and oppression before they have a chance to spread. For example, if something like the Marshall Plan had been initiated following the First World War, the Second World War might never have happened. As the lines I often repeat from Wallace Stevens tell us:

> *After the final no there comes a yes,*
> *and on that yes the future world depends.*

And so it is in our personal lives. We can and must say *no* to abuse and meanness, and to our own unfriendliness toward ourselves, but even that *no* has its roots in our love for life and for the well-being of all. Our everyday work must be to water those roots. There are many ways we can do this, most of them quite small and intimate — practicing kindness, forbearance, patience — but the most profound way is by opening our hearts to the nature of Pure Presence (or whatever name we wish to call it).

This is the gift of the mystic path. In its essence it is not a complicated path, but it asks of us complete openness and release of self-concepts, opinions, and judgment. To the extent we can open our hearts to the nature of Pure Presence we realize that its nature is love, a love that is light-years beyond what we usually consider that little word to signify. It is unconditional. It's the love that flames the stars and spins every atom. It's the gift of this beginningless, endless moment, the infinite generosity of now. When we recognize that this love is at the root of our own nature and the nature of all being — even though it is so often eclipsed by fear in the human realm — we open ourselves to its unshakable power.

Faith-Mind

THE TITLE OF THE *HSIN HSIN Ming*, the enigmatic 6th century text from the Chan tradition, is typically translated as: *Verses on Absolute Trust*, or *Engraving Trust in the Heart*, or *Verses on the Faith-Mind*, along with other variations. The meaning of "trust" or "faith" here is not intended as belief in a religious conception of some kind — belief or faith in God, Allah, Buddha, or any religious narrative — it is a *faith* so intimate that there is no intervention of a storyline or icon upon which to have faith. Similarly, the word "mind" in the title refers not to our rational mind but to awareness itself, the immediate *heart-presence* of our nature.

The text of the *Hsin Hsin Ming* takes this even further when it says: Faith and mind are not two. Not-two is faith-mind.

Faith-mind. What is it? How can we realize it? In a way, our faith-mind is already present in us right now and there's nothing we need to do to make it happen. We have faith that the breath we are breathing this moment will occur by itself and will provide us with the oxygen we need to live. We have faith that we can understand these words. If we reach for a cup of tea, we have faith that our hand will find the teacup handle without difficulty.

The fundamental nature of faith-mind doesn't imply that outer forms of religious faith are false.

In our not-so-easy immersion into human being-ness, religious faith can be a profound support as we seek to release our fears, self-preoccupation, and sense of separation. But finally, awakening from the dream of separation, the particulars of religious narratives vanish. All naming ceases. It must. Face to face with God, there is no God, no me, no you.

This is how I understand faith-mind. It's immediate and inherent in the moment. As many of you who are reading this know well, opening to the nature of faith-mind happens spontaneously as we learn to relax the sense of being a "me" — the one who likes this and doesn't like that, the one who has opinions, the one who wants to be a better person, the one who wants to be respected, seen, or who wants to matter. In fact, faith-mind is exactly what allows us to relax from this identification and simply be present in the present moment, without attachment to memories, thoughts, hopes or fears — just here. We realize that our presence happens all by itself, and we can have faith in that. This is faith-mind. Absolute trust.

From this space of simple, unadorned presence, we know we're safe. Indeed, there's no "me" to be safe or unsafe. We simply *are* faith-mind.

I realize this kind of talk can sound a bit other-worldly, abstract, and disconnected from our daily concerns, but that's not the nature of faith-mind. Think of the faith-mind of Han-Shan, the crazy-wisdom mountain poet who lived at about the same time that the *Hsin Hsin Ming* was written. In his poems he tells how he simply lets heaven and earth go about their changes, he lets the sounds of nature purify his ears, he doesn't worry or fear. He's at ease with following his karma through, finished with a tangled, hung-up mind, writing his poems, laughing with his old monk friend Shih-te, taking whatever comes. His faith-mind is natural and uncomplicated. He knows he's *safe*.

What does that mean – safe?

It means that he knows, all the way through his faith-mind, that this spacious awake presence we are is not something that comes and goes. It's the very nature of reality, and we are insepa-rable from it. Old Han Shan was no different from us. Like him, we too can wander at ease, effortless and fearless in the assurance of faith-mind. The universe's spontaneity is ours. Like him, we are connected to everything, whole. The body of the universe is our body.

We can wander in this life with the faith-mind of a Han Shan, a Buddha, a Jesus, a free woman, a free man. We can love and care for this beautiful world and all its beings with compassion and tenderness, with a happy, carefree heart. Faith-mind is ours — not-two!

I know that when I carry on like this, there's often a little "but" that sails into peoples' minds: **But** I'm NOT safe, not really – so many terrible things could happen – my children could get hurt or die, my house could burn down, I could lose everything that I love!

Yes, that's true. Anything can happen and we know it. A terminal diagnosis could come tomorrow. Pain, sickness, and death are just a roll of the dice away.

So how can we speak of being safe, of living in faith-mind without fear? Is it really possible? Is there some magic to protect us? No, there's no magic, there's nothing to protect us from loss. As we know all too well: everyone we love, everything we value, everything we have ever been given — our bodies, our parents and children, our friends, comforts, good works, this beautiful natural world — all of it will one day be taken from us.

That's how it is here. There's a sadness that comes with this life that we can't avoid, nor should we try. It's the cello sound of that which we love, passing. If we resist knowing that sadness, we diminish our lives. When we don't resist it, when our faith-mind allows the cello's melody into our souls, our lives win a measure of fineness and depth, a nobility even — the quiet nobility of being mortal.

But of course, this tender sadness that comes with living and loving is not the whole story. In the end, thankfulness transcends grief. The great honor of being human and to have been given all these chances to love is evidence of something wholly good that's inherent in this moment and in the nature of reality, and our faith-mind knows it.

The Practice of
Not Knowing

WALKING ON A MOUNTAIN TRAIL ON an early winter morning,
I came upon a large rock where I could sit awhile and rest. Patches
of snow lay under the pinion pines; the sun hadn't found them yet.
A sparkle caught my eye — a drop of water forming at the tip of
a pine needle near me — meltwater coming from a little clump of
snow higher up the branch. The drop slowly grew fatter, glistening in the sunlight, and then let go. Another drop began to form.

I had just been marveling about the mysterious capacity of my
mind to know things — how my mind can distinguish this tree
from that tree, and how it's able to name them and know something about what they are. It *was* marvelous, and yet — could it
be that the very skill of naming and knowing was also limiting
my experience — of the things of the world, of other people, of
the Real — in ways that were invisible to me?

I watched the next drop of water form on the tip of the pine needle. *What is this, this drop of water? What is it?* Of course, I knew its name and that it came from melting snow, that came from the clouds, that came from... I knew about the whole hydrologic cycle, I knew water was made up of hydrogen and oxygen, but... *what is it, really?*

I didn't know. It was a mystery to me, how it could be what it is and not something else, or where it had been or where it was going. I realized I didn't know anything about its origins as water or its age or destiny, or how its essence performed all the magic that water is capable of. What *was* its essence? Did it have one?

I looked up at the tree. All by itself, my bewilderment about the nature of the little drop of water expanded to include the tree. *What is this, this "tree?"* Do I know? And the forest it's part of? *What is it?*

I looked around. Everything looked like it normally did — trees, rocks, patches of snow, the careless jumble of the forest — and yet there was something else, something appearing out of my bewilderment about the nature of these presences I was with — a sense of them that was both vivid and indescribable. Asking *what is it?* and admitting I didn't know, seemed to relax my mind's hold on things. My mind became humble and a little shy. It stopped trying to be first.

What arrived in its place, this "indescribable vividness," felt familiar in the way a home-place feels familiar, ordinary, and natural. Though I didn't really know what the drop of water was, or the tree, or the forest, I belonged with them. Instead of my internal commentary and "knowings," there was a kind of clear spaciousness that we shared, a wholeness.

The forest was still full of forest sounds, yet it was silent and spacious. My body was still full of sensations, yet it too was silent and spacious. Everything was present, together.

It didn't take long before I wondered: *What about God, the Divine, the Real? What is It? What is all This?* Though I've spent a lifetime with these questions, in that moment of asking I had to admit *I don't know.*

"Not knowing is most intimate," says the turning phrase of a Zen koan. *Not knowing is most intimate.* Intimacy may be the best word to describe what is revealed when the mind gets shy like this — the intimacy of "two" being connected *without twoness*, while remaining distinctly two.

I remembered the famous prayer of Mohammed's that's always seemed a little odd to me: *"Oh Lord, increase my perplexity concerning Thee!"* Perplexity, bewilderment, uncertainty, not knowing — these words that usually imply a disturbing state of mind to be overcome are inviting us into a different kind of "knowing" beyond the mind's assertions. "The whole affair of God," writes Ibn Arabi, "is perplexity."

Most of the attempts of the world's mystical traditions that try to describe the Divine, the One, the Real, the Dharmakaya, revert to *paradox* or to the negation of any assertion — leaving us in a state of perplexity. When Ramana Maharshi asked someone, *Who are you?* he would respond to any answer with the words, *Neti neti,* "not that, not that." The Buddha, pointing to the nature of things, said, *Not two. Not one.* The remembrance (*zikr*) of Sufis, *la ilaha ila'llah,* means "No God but God." The positive or *cataphatic* theologies that assert God's attributes and qualities (God is good, etc.,) were inevitably met with negative or *apophatic* theologies — *apophatic*, a word that literally means "*to un-say God.*"

Not knowing, as a practice, is a move that's always available to us. When I look at a mountain and ask, *What is it?* and admit I don't really know what its mountain-ness is, the humility of that admission lets me be in its presence in a new way. When I meet someone and ask, *Who is she, really? Who is he, really?* and admit I don't truly know who this being is or what has created them to be what they are, I become open to their presence in a new way.

A spaciousness comes, a lightness of being that brings with it a sense of amazement and awe — *what is this water drop, this person, this moment, this awareness of awareness?* In the absence of answers comes wonder! Soon the questions themselves vanish. This is why Chan Buddhists describe this *practice of not knowing*, of perplexity, as *wonderment*. A gentle unfolding of experience in wonderment. Perhaps when we were little children we could access wonderment without having to ask what a thing was or admit we didn't know; our minds were not yet so dominant or so focused on survival. Older now, with all our predispositions of knowing and judging and opinion-making, we can be happy to play with this simple practice of not knowing, asking *What is it?* — and not know.

The Practice of
Living Presence

THE ZEN MASTER KATAGIRI ROSHI ONCE said to his students:

> In order to have warm human relations, we must pay
> attention to what is. In other words, we must touch the
> source of existence. Only then can we take a deep breath;
> only then can we feel relief. Under all circumstances, we
> must be rooted in the source of existence.

What does it mean to be *rooted in the source of existence*? What
is this source and how can we know it?

In my experience, being rooted in the source of existence does
not involve the thought-mind or require concentration. What is
required is more like an intuitive openness, perhaps compara-
ble to our peripheral vision or our experience of spatial dimensions. It's a subtle capacity we have, to be able to open ourselves

intuitively like this. For me it has a kinesthetic feel to it, as if the back of my head has disappeared, or the space inside my chest has no boundary.

So to benefit from what the Zen master said — *under all circumstances, we must be rooted in the source of existence* — we will need to allow our intuitive capacity to spread its wings, and not just try to understand conceptually what he's saying.

The source of existence is immanently *present*, and it is *alive*.

Everything we see and feel, including the intimate and ever-changing feelings of our body and the thoughts we think, is inseparable from the source of existence. It is not that there is a source over here making existence over there, or that a source in the past made existence happen now. Existence and its source are immediate; they are happening all at once, and that happening is *alive*. I'm not referring to carbon-based life here, but to the immanence and impulse and creative becoming-ness that we experience moment to moment as the dynamic of reality.

Existence as we know it is continually changing and moving. It is alive with itself. Quarks appear out of nowhere, light blossoms from stars, our eyes move across the page, cars on the street roll by — everything is flowing forth magically, becoming what has never been before.

To the extent that we can appreciate this *aliveness* we root ourselves in the source of existence. Again, this is not an intellectual appreciation but an intuitive openness to how everything we perceive shares this blessed aliveness in this moment.

Simultaneous with *aliveness* and its ever-changing nature, is a numinous, ineffable stillness I call *presence* (it also has many other names.) *Presence* is the silent host of all that appears. It is what allows *aliveness* to flow forth. One way to intuit what I mean by *presence* is through the analogy of space. Space allows things to show up. If there were no space there would be no possibility for chair, table, or our bodies to appear as they do. *Presence* is like that, but is even more mysterious since it's not dimensional in the way we imagine space to be, and yet it is everywhere.

Presence is silence itself, perfectly clear, open, and contentless. It may be difficult for us to understand how these apparent opposites — aliveness and stillness, sound and silence, co-arise as the source of existence, but they do. It's like what happens when we listen. Our listening is silent, and that silence allows us to hear sounds. In the same way, our most intimate awareness is silent, pure, and clear, and that silent clarity allows existence to appear.

How marvelous, the presence of everything that we perceive, that is alive and changing, is simultaneously still, silent, and unchanging! Inayat Khan speaks of this primordial silence: *"...our eyes cannot see it and our ears cannot hear it and our mind cannot perceive it because it is beyond mind, thought, and comprehension."* In this same passage he describes beautifully how we awaken to the silent quality at the source of existence:

> *This all-pervading, unbroken, inseparable, unlimited, ever-present, omnipotent silence unites with our silence like the meeting of flames.*

The Great Silent Presence and our own silent presence meet,

and though they were never separate, experiencing their meeting is what roots us in the source of existence.

Katagiri Roshi begins his instruction with the words, "Under all circumstances" — *Under all circumstances, we must be rooted in the source of existence.* That's a tall order. Again and again circumstances find us oblivious to the source of existence, caught up in odd assumptions about what is real and what matters. We need help here. We need to discover ways that we can easily remind ourselves of the *living presence* that is the source of existence.

To that end, below is an outline of a simple practice that might be helpful. In this version I use breathing as the sensory focal point; you can experiment with other sensations once you get comfortable with the practice. Then you can do it while walking down the street, or eating a meal, or in the midst of a conversation. Having done something like this practice for a few years, I've found that over time it's become less step-by-step as in this outline, and more fluid and creative. Whereas the practice here takes several minutes, eventually you may find it happens in a few seconds and becomes the kind of effortless kinesthetic movement I mentioned earlier. Good luck!

The Practice of Living Presence

1. *Sit quietly. Come to rest, body and mind relaxed and alert.*
2. *Bring your attention to your breath. Breathe naturally.*
3. *With your attention on the living, changing nature*

*of your breath, simultaneously open your awareness
to the presence in which your breath rises and falls.*

4. *Effortlessly allow your awareness of presence to open
to the boundless presence in which your surround-
ings appear, and in which your body and its sensations, thoughts, and feelings appear.*

5. *Notice that everything that appears moves, everything that arises comes and goes, while presence
doesn't. Recognizing movement in stillness, sound in
silence, living presence: this is the key point.*

The Middle of the Sky — A Practice

AT THE HEART OF SUFI PRAXIS is the recurrent theme called *fana*, often translated as "annihilation of the self." A better translation might be *"releasing identification with the <u>sense</u> of self,"* for the "self" is not something that actually exists. As Ibn 'Arabi points out, *"How can a thing that does not exist try to get rid of its existence? How could a thing that is not, become nothing?"*

In "Selflessness" (p. 73), I suggested a simple practice for recognizing our innate absence of self: *Simply be present, right now.* When you can relax knowingly in the present moment you interrupt the habit of assembling a "self" — "You're just here, without being you."

Admittedly, our recognition in these clear moments usually only lasts a few seconds before we assume our identity again as the "me" who narrates its thought-stream and who may feel beleaguered by its litany of emotions and old traumas. Yet even these short reprieves can serve to relax the habit of situating ourselves as a separate "self." As the saying goes, "Little moments, many times."

Another practice in this vein, also deceptively simple, I call "the Middle of the Sky." I've taken this phrase from a passage in one of Keith Dowman's extraordinary books (*Dzogchen Busuku*) in which he describes the experience of emerging from profound contemplation of intrinsic presence. At that moment, he writes, *"our experience is like the middle of the sky..."*

This little phrase, *"like the middle of the sky,"* can offer our crowded minds an immediate, spontaneous recognition — a remembrance — of our true nature. It's not complicated. It doesn't require repetition or any manipulation of our consciousness. Simply take a moment and see that your present-moment "self" — your being in the moment — is like the middle of the sky: clear, non-located, spacious, and undefinable. There's no need to do anything with that recognition, or to make it more than it is, or to understand it.

You may experience this as having a slight kinesthetic quality — as if the space behind your eyes is like the middle of the sky... and your heart center, and each breath entering your body — *the middle of the sky*. Clear, non-located, spacious, and undefinable.

Then let it be. Relax any attempt to maintain or repeat whatever you experience as "the middle of the sky." This is a subtle place for all of us — we experience a moment of freedom from the illusion of self and we get attached to that experience, we want more of it. Just let it be.

Then, occasionally, when your mind gets crowded with self-thoughts and with emotional pressures and judgments, you may remember this phrase — *the middle of the sky* — and it may once again open the window of your being to the fresh morning air that you are.

The Welcoming Practice

THE WELCOMING PRACTICE IS A FUSION of guidance from several mystical traditions: Christianity, Sufism, Zen, Advaita, and Dzogchen in particular. It has its most direct antecedents in the Christian *Centering Prayer* practice as developed by a number of Catholic mystics (Merton, Keating, Menninger, Pennington, Bourgeault, and others) inspired by the 14th century text *The Cloud of Unknowing* and the practices of earlier desert ascetics. However, this Welcoming Practice is a distinct variation drawing from the praxis of several traditions, which is one reason I've started calling it the Welcoming Practice — it welcomes these various forms of guidance that are united in their devotion to the same mystery.

The Welcoming Practice has three aspects which I call: *Bow Inside; Consent to Silence;* and *Welcome Love.* Though I'll describe them here in sequence, you may find that when you engage in this practice these three aspects mingle and occur within and through each other, and are not as separate as they might sound in this description.

Bow Inside

When you sit down to begin your meditation practice, very likely a sense of your self-identity sits down with you. Since it's your "self-identity" — what you believe yourself to be — it can be hard to spot. To "bow inside" means to relinquish whatever that identity is by a simple move of humility — the bow — to open yourself directly to the simple presence you are. No decorations, no stories, just your clear presence in the moment. As an early Sufi advised, *"Put your forehead on the prayer mat and don't presume."*

The "move" of *bowing inside* isn't a physical movement, although it can have a kinaesthetic feel to it. Like a physical bow, this bow is a move toward self-effacement and unpretentiousness, a giving-over of one's insularity: *"Take me away from myself!"* as Ibn Arabi cries in his beautiful prayer. To *bow inside* means to offer yourself in all humility, in your simple presence, during the sacred moments of this practice. Just your clear presence, nothing more.

In her wonderful descriptions of Centering Prayer, Cynthia Bourgeault points to a single line in *The Cloud of Unknowing* that suggests the essence of what I mean by bowing inside: it is to have, as the anonymous author of *The Cloud* writes: *"Naked intent direct to God."* It is this "nakeding" that is the interior bow, an unclothing of your personhood to its simplicity and readiness, for in this practice you are inviting "God" to be with you, to open yourself to the unspeakable mystery of the numinous. To welcome its presence you cannot come adorned with self-identity; you have to come naked. Here you may wish to replace the word "God" with some other signifier that means the same thing — *Naked intent direct to Pure Awareness,* or *Naked intent direct to Buddha Nature,* or *Naked intent direct to Silence.*

CONSENT TO SILENCE

"Consent to silence" is Father Thomas Keating's concise instruction for this process of "nakeding." To consent is to allow, to open to the openness that is silent, that is the background of every moment of our lives. One way to *consent* in this way is to recognize that our very capacity to listen is silent. Whatever listening is, it is silent. This is why the Advaita nondual teacher Jean Klein advises, *"Listen to listening."* We recognize that pure awareness itself is silence. God is silence. Or in Meister Eckhart's words, "Silence is God's first language."

Now to the degree you have managed to *bow inside* and to *consent to silence,* you will soon experience distractions, mostly in the form of thoughts, or perhaps images, emotive currents or bodily sensations that draw your interested attention toward them. This is not a failure. In a way, it's the heart of this practice, for each thought or sensation that attracts your attention gives you a chance to let it go, to *relax the tension* that your attention fixes upon it. That relaxing is the key. It will present itself as an opportunity again and again. Each time you notice you've attached your attention to some property that appears, relax. Consent to silence. As Zen master Dainin Katagiri points out, "... just put aside all kinds of imagination fabricated by your consciousness. Don't attach to thoughts and emotions; just let them return to emptiness."

Let the silence swallow them up. Consenting to silence means letting whatever has captured your attention return to emptiness. You don't have to do anything to make this happen. As it is pointed out in Dzogchen texts: *"All thoughts are self-liberated."* They vanish by themselves as soon as you relax your interest in them. This is why Sufi Inayat Khan called meditation *mystical relaxation.*

Welcome Love

At first I hesitated to use the word "love" to describe this aspect of the practice, since love is a word that so easily can seem sentimental or denote personal affection. In saying that, I don't mean to disparage sentiment or affection — praise them! They are human resonances of the "divine" love that gives us this moment that blossoms everywhere as everything. To *welcome love* in the context of this practice means to welcome in our hearts a glimpse of this divine love — though again, to use the word "divine" may be just as perilous as using the word "love," for it seems to imply a divinity or entity from which love is dispensed, and then we are caught in thinking dualistically about what is in essence not dualistic. *Divine love is the radiance of Being*, not something that issues forth from a God that is made into something separate in our minds.

But how can we welcome this vast, unspeakable love? Happily, it emerges by itself and welcomes us to the degree that we have consented to silence, which means we can't make it happen through our insistence. And yet, "we can put ourselves in the way of it," as Ibn Arabi tells us. Here we can take to heart an instruction from Plotinus, speaking of the same unspeakable love:

> *Let those who are unfamiliar with this state imagine, on the basis of their loves here down below, what it must be like to encounter the being they love most of all.*

"Imagine what it must be like..." — that's where we can start, in the imagination of the heart, not the mind. By grace such imagination breaks us loose from conceptions of love, and then divine love like an awesome wind takes over. Here we can no longer talk in prose — Sufis are especially enamoured of this kind of love poetry, and the 11th century Persian Sufi Abdullah Ansari, in his *Book of Love*, goes so far as to say Sufism is simply another word for love:

> *Love is the mark of the Tribe, the title of the Tariqah (Way)... It has three degrees:*
> *The first degree is a love that cuts off disquieting thoughts, makes service enjoyable, and offers solace in afflictions...*

> *The second degree is a love that incites preferring the Real to all else, elicits remembrance on the tongue, and attaches the heart to witnessing it…*
>
> *The third degree is a dazzling love that cuts off express-ing, makes allusions subtle, and does not reach descrip-tion. This love is the pivot of this business…*

I quote these love words to remind us that in this *Welcoming Practice* what we are inviting ourselves to be in the presence of is so awesome, sacred, and of a radiant, loving mystery so unknow-able that we can only *bow inside*. To me, this practice has the capacity to take us beyond the quiet composure of recognizing nondual awareness — it passes through that doorway, yes — and then reveals to us a loving sacredness that is at the same time infinitely awesome and purely intimate.

World Worry

A DISTURBING LITANY OF DISASTERS CONFRONTS us in most observant writings these days, and for good reason: *our planet and human civilization are encountering conditions in which the earth's capacity for nourishing life is endangered at a magnitude unknown in human history.* You know the litany: polar bears lost on melting ice floes, songbirds vanishing, soil depleted, poisons in the air and our bodies, countless trillions of plastic fragments floating in the oceans, forests burning and diseased, extractive industries gouging into mountains, a fierce ambition in human economies to grow past all limits, populations of refugees fleeing from social and climate disruption, and ever-increasing injustice, distrust, polarization, and domination of the many by the few. All of this is stirring in us *world worry,* a sense of foreboding that is draining the vibrancy of human culture as well as our physical, psychological, and spiritual health. We see a menacing cloud over the future and feel helpless to do anything about it.

World worry is not something we can avoid. Even if we try to shut it out and just devote ourselves to the demands and plea-sures of our personal lives, the storm gathering over us and over our children and their children is a portent we can't ignore for long. While we may realize that world worry is sapping the en-ergy from our lives, at the same time we feel *if we don't worry* about what's coming down, we'll take no action to forestall it. Releasing our world worry would mean giving in, giving up.

How can we be with this? What *is* our responsibility in this fateful time? What is asked of us?

And then there's this troubling question: *Can we be awake to the enormous ecological and social disruption that's happening now and that's ever increasing — disruption that, I repeat, is on a scale that no generation before us has had to face — can we be awake to it and still live happy, beautiful and fulfilled lives?*

There are no easy answers to these questions, and no easy fixes. As the days and years pass, each of us will have to contend with this intractable challenge in a manner suited to our own lives. Here are a few thoughts of my own in response to these questions — culled down to three basic "principles" — offered not as definitive answers, but more as a starting point for your own contemplation and questioning.

Keep an Undefended Heart

In my own life I try to accept my world worry not as a looming horror that makes me want to shut down, but as a "necessary angel" that keeps my heart open. For example, at the moment I'm aware of the 900,000 Syrian refugees escaping the fighting

Pir Elias Amidon

in northwestern Syria; many are without shelter, huddled in the freezing weather. I've been to Syria many times and I feel connected to those people. Though I know I can't really imagine the desperation of a father or a mother trying to keep their children from freezing, or the scale of suffering there (900,000 people!) and everywhere in the world, I know if I close my heart to it, my own life and the greater life I am part of will be diminished. Even though I'm in no position to do anything about their suffering, that very helplessness becomes part of theirs... and somehow within it we share a mutual presence. My helpless caring matters.

I wonder if the extreme of world worry, when we become overwhelmed by the anxiety of knowing the earth's life-support systems are collapsing, isn't in itself a kind of defense, a way to defend our hearts from being present. Being overwhelmed, we curl into anticipatory grief and the certainty that everything's hopeless.

I think here of the prayer-words of Etty Hillesum a year before she was murdered at Auschwitz:

> These are times of terror, my God. Tonight for the first time I stayed awake in the dark, my eyes burning, images of human suffering parading endlessly before me. I am going to promise you one thing, my God, oh, a trifle: I will not let myself weigh down the present day with those fears that the future inspires in me...

Those are the words of an undefended heart, open to the hurt of the world without letting that hurt crush her heart's presence.

124

An undefended heart is in this way the requisite condition for survival, maybe not physical survival but survival of the most noble aspect of the human spirit. If, in the end, the earth's human experiment does fail, at least we will have succumbed with our hearts alive and loving.

FIND WHAT MATTERS

When we experience our world worry not through the lens of fear but through our undefended heart, something very intimate changes in us. Our life comes closer. Worry and despair open into compassion. Our undefended heart reveals to us that we *are* the world, undivided from it. Then, in the moments of our lives, we do our best to be faithful to what matters. As the novelist Barbara Kingsolver once remarked, *"In a world as wrong as this one, all we can do is make things as right as we can."*

Making things "right," in however small a way, asks that we discover, in each life situation we encounter, *what matters*. Finding what matters isn't an intellectual exercise, like making a list. It's more alive than that, more immediate to our moment-to-moment experience. For example, we might say that "kindness matters," but the living quality of kindness is something that we must find and open to, again and again, as we live.

Given time, this "finding what matters" becomes a natural, intuitive move. It doesn't need to be thought about, although sometimes thinking can help us remember what's at stake. Say you find yourself getting irritable about something — at the moment that you notice your irritability you might ask yourself, "What really matters here?" This question might come verbally like this, or it may be a subtle shift in your heart. Either way, it creates a pause, and in that pause you make things as right as you can.

In my own life I experience this process of "finding what matters" in the day-to-day situations that arise — in how I respond to and care for others, care for my household, care for my health, care for the work I do. In fact, finding what matters is the very yoga I try to follow as I write this essay and look for the next sentence or word. *What matters here?* In an earlier part of my life when I designed houses for a living, the same questioning guided my design process — what matters here? What is the life that wants to happen here? How can this design be faithful to that?

But finding what matters isn't only something that's active in the details of our lives, it can also guide us in their larger trajectory — what work we turn to, how we determine our life's priorities, and what we give our energy to. Here our question about "what matters" resonates deep into the future, not only in our own lives but into the lives of our descendants, into the seventh generation. How will what I devote my life to nourish the life that is to come?

But whether in the details of our lives or in the fundamental directions our lives take, *finding and following what matters* is the very current that will heal the world. We can be sure of that.

Do the Beautiful

Following what matters is the essence of the Sufi principle of *ihsan,* which translates as *doing the beautiful.* When Dostoyevsky wrote, *"Beauty will save the world,"* he was saying, among other things, that *beauty matters*. Here beauty is not simply understood as something that has an aesthetically pleasing appearance. The beautiful act — *doing the beautiful* — is an act that *fits* what a situation calls for, an act that arises spontaneously when the heart recognizes what matters. The beautiful act nourishes and calls forth the life that is nascent in a situation.

Doing the beautiful doesn't come about from thinking or planning. It happens naturally to the degree we have devoted our life to "undefending" our heart and finding what matters. *"Let the beauty you love be what you do,"* Rumi famously told us, an advice we cannot remember too often. In the context of transforming our *world worry* — our concern for the perilous condition of the planet and human civilization — into a path of healing, I cannot think of a more succinct instruction.

Here we might find an answer to the question: *Can we be awake to the enormous ecological and social disruption that's happening now and that's ever increasing, and still live happy, beautiful and fulfilled lives?* I believe this is exactly what we must do. I don't have any illusions about the suffering and loss we are witnessing today, or the magnitude of the threats facing the community of life on earth in the future. But if a world abundant with life is to be seeded by us, it will not grow from anxiety or despair; it will only thrive in the fertile soil of our undefended hearts, finding — and doing — what is beautiful.

Sufi Tao

A YOUNG SEEKER ONCE ASKED AN old Sufi woman, "Mother, tell me, what is the way of the Sufi? What way do you follow?" She replied:

The way we follow does not lead.
It is like a wind that has no origin
and that seeks no destination.
It flows everywhere without moving,
never straying from this moment.
The way we follow is holy and alive
but to call it a way is to make it a thought,
suitable for the mind but not the heart.

The love-wind we follow teaches without instruction.
It reveals a path without pointing.
Accepting what arises, it holds on to nothing,

holding on to nothing it embraces all things.
Following the way, one is gentle
and does not defend or claim to know.
Not knowing,
one goes the way in wonder.

The way has no abode yet it is home.
In the evening friends gather and sing.
At dawn they go their own way without leaving.
Having no abode they are free.
Free, they are unafraid of rejection and death.
Unafraid, they give comfort to the comfortless.
If someone asks them who they are,
they say, a friend.

The way we follow does not separate or declare,
nor does it draw attention to itself.
Loving, it has no need to possess.
Intimate, its secret remains secret.
Though it is most holy, it is not special.
It belongs to all beings and is never withheld.
No one and nothing is outside of the way,
but few know it.

To know the way is to be the way.
Kind, the way is naturally kind.
Curious, it laughs with amazement.

Pir Elias Amidon

If you do not know the way, be kind.
If you do not know the way, be curious.
Then like a leaf warmed in the sun,
in autumn you will turn gold, then brittle,
then earth, and never stop living.

STORIES

Morning Light:
Five Scenes

UPSTATE NEW YORK, USA

All night there have been cricket sounds in the field. Now they stop. A stillness touches everything, like when a conductor raises his baton and the orchestra goes silent. Dawn begins, pale blue, coral, faint gold. The first solitary birdsong sails up, and then others from here and there join as the last stars vanish. A great expectancy fills the air. Finally, suddenly, a brilliance pierces the edge of the hill, and without hurry the sun lifts above it. Down at the edge of the field where blackberries make a tangle of stems and thorns, a young rabbit sits quietly, only her nose twitching as she breathes in the smells of the morning. She watches as the faraway sun enters a dewdrop on a blade of grass. Inside her body her little heart beats unnoticed.

Valparaíso, Chile

In the hospital the old man lies in his bed, his head turned toward the window. His breathing is shallow. He can see the top branches of a tree and the pale blue of the dawn sky beyond them. He waits quietly, without waiting for anything. Now the first piece of sunlight touches the window frame. He watches as it slowly stretches across the wall. The man's disappointment with how things have turned out drifts away. He feels himself becoming lighter, buoyant, as if he is being held by something greater than gravity.

Hill Tribe Village, Northwest Thailand

The twelve-year-old girl lifts the bucket slowly from behind the sack of grain so it doesn't wake anyone. Her little body knows how to move through the crowded space of the hut without disturbing her sleeping family, stepping carefully between the different sounds of their breathing. Once outside and free of the porch and its two steps, she moves lightly down the path, swinging the bucket as if it was her little brother's hand. Then at the creek she bends to fill it and, looking up, sees the first white spark of sunlight through the trees, watching her.

Near Hyderabad, India

In the gray light before sunrise the young man waits with the other laborers on the platform as the heavy train to Hyderabad hisses into the station and comes to a stop. Like every morning, the train is already full, men and women leaning out from the windows and doors, holding on. He climbs up the rungs at the back of a car and sits on the roof with a dozen others. The train lurches and pulls itself out of the station. This is the part of the day he likes the best, nothing to carry, the wind on his face, watching the mist on the paddies turn golden as the first sunlight spreads down the valley. The train clatters along, carrying his quiet eyes to a day of work.

Avignon, France

The woman wakes before he does, the dawn light pale on the ceiling. She feels happy without knowing that's what she's feeling. She turns on her side and from under the sheets comes the faint smell of their lovemaking still on her skin. She lies still, watching how the first beam of sunlight through the window makes mountain ranges and valleys on the rumpled sheets. She imagines herself finding her way among them, like a pilgrim.

~

Dawn

HERE IN THE MOUNTAINS JUST BEFORE dawn, the air is mo-
tionless. It feels as if the world has stopped breathing. The first
faint blue light comes so quietly over the eastern peaks that nothing is disturbed below. Nothing moves. The stalks of the wild
grasses stand perfectly still. The branches of the junipers and
pinions are poised in the air, waiting. The long night bows to the
coming of the day.

Now the dark and the light are intimate. One dissolves into
the other like lovers do. Together they're in awe. Though the dark
and the light have touched like this for countless rounds, it's always new for them. Here in the penumbra where they are not
one or the other, they share their secrets; the mystic night tells of
its immensity, and the daylight tells of each particular. How they
love each other! As their love-play circles the planet, caressing it,
blessing it, it is always somewhere, always approaching, always
welcoming, always leaving, anointing the world.

Nearby, a coyote lifts her head. And out in the valley, in a farmhouse, a woman draws open the curtains in her children's bedroom, the sound of the opening curtains meant to wake them. She pauses, looking out east to the blue mountains and the coral light above.

The coyote stretches.

The eldest boy gets up and dresses without speaking. He goes to the kitchen and fills a bucket with water to take out to the shed for his new little goat. He pulls on his boots, his denim jacket, takes the bucket in hand and crosses the yard, the air cool and still.

The coyote looks up. The coral light of the dawn now has gold streaks through it. In the west the last few star-sparks are vanishing. In that moment, whatever it is that rises from the coyote's heart makes her lift her nose to the sky and sing one long, wavering note.

The boy stops in the middle of the yard, tilts his head. What was that? He stands still, listening. Now he sees the quiet glory in the sky above him. An unexpected feeling comes over him, a feeling he hasn't felt before but that's somehow wholly familiar. It's as if the ground beneath his boots and the pink sky above the barnyard and the electric light from the kitchen window and the shuffling of the cows in the barn and him standing there, bucket in hand, all belong, all at once, together, like in some great loving hymn of home.

The coyote cries out once more. This time the boy recognizes what it is. He tilts his head back and hollers out in answer, *Ohwoooo!*

One Love

I ONCE ASKED MY MOTHER WHEN she was washing dishes at the sink, "Mommy, who do you love more, Daddy or us kids?"

She paused in her washing and said, "Ducky, love doesn't come in quantities. It just touches us in different ways."

It's taken a long time but now I know what she meant. She was right — you can't have more or less of love. For example, it's not like time — you can have a lot of time, or you can run out of it. Love isn't like that. Love is more like the present moment, like now. You can't have "more now" or "less now," can you? Right now?

Or perhaps we could say it's like what is looking out of our eyes. Can we have more or less of that? What is it that is looking, or listening to the sounds around us? Did the Buddha have more of that than we do? What is it? Does whatever it is come in quantities?

My son left a phone message last night that I just picked up. He ended by saying, "Sending you lots of love." Lots. A friend of mine always concludes his emails with the salutation, "Big love." We want to tell each other we really mean it, so we turn to words that emphasize scale. How dear we are! And what else can we do? We're trying to express something that escapes definition.

My sense is that love is like an invisible light that continuously ignites our being and all being everywhere. Love is the very radiance of each moment's becoming — it's that generous. That may sound abstract, but it's actually so intimate and immediate we don't know we know it, like the story of the little fish who doesn't know what the ocean is.

Love is how and why emptiness bursts forth as form, how clear presence shows up as all these myriad presences. It's the impulse of universal becoming, the élan vital, what Buddhists call the *sambhogakaya*, the clear, luminous presence that gifts all manifestation — your existence, my existence, the earth spinning, all of it given fresh every instant.

When we feel love for someone or something it's as if a channel opens in our heart to this great love that's at the beginning of everything. At its source it's unconditional. Once we start layering conditions on it, well, then the channel narrows into likes and dislikes. This is why my teacher, Murshid Fazal Inayat-Khan, said, *"You can always love more."* Not more in quantity but in embrace. When our heart opens in love it doesn't stop with a single love object — wherever we turn we see with the eyes of love.

To see with the eyes of love doesn't mean that we are blind to the meanness and violence of the world. The infinite love I'm speaking of, the love beyond all ideas of quantity, is not blind. It sees all, knows all, embraces all. This is not something that's easily understood with our normal way of perceiving the world, and it's certainly beyond the scope of these words. Perhaps all we might appreciate here is how our recognition of the world's injustice, ignorance, and brutality functions for us as a teacher — it shows us what matters, what we care about, what is worth saving.

> We listen to the news and don't approve.
> Things are worse than we thought.
> Though that may be, may we never forget
> the love our pain is faithful to.

My mother's instruction to me about love concluded with the words: *It just touches us in different ways.* Of course, this is obvious, but it may help us to see how *love can appear in so many guises and still be one.* It's like water — here it's a raindrop, here an ocean, here a tear, here it flows in the veins of a bird in flight, here it makes possible each movement of our bodies. One love!

Of all the guidance I have received in my life, the guidance of love is the most reliable. It's not always easy to follow — self-pity, disappointment, and outrage can obscure love's path — but when the dust clears, love is what remains. To the extent we can open ourselves to the one love, the love without quantity, our lives become beautiful and of benefit, part of the great gift of now.

Easter Egg

ON A FESTIVE DAY WHEN I was three I found a lavender egg beneath a tree. It was Easter and the air was full of morning and the sun was shining, little children were running about, and then all of a sudden something happened, something that's actually the first memory of my life.

I saw (and in that moment everything became quiet, at least in my memory it was quiet) I saw a glint of lavender in the leaves beneath a tree — a lavender egg half-covered by brown leaves nestled in the bosom roots of a tree that went way up into the sky.

It was so quiet, though the children were squealing in the front yard, and in the silence my small hand reached out, and I knew, I felt, something magical was happening, something intensely beautiful was being born from the dark beneath the leaves out of where the tree grew and the darkness down there began.

I took the egg into my fingers and touched its perfect seamless shape. Egg. Lavender egg. I held it to my cheek. It was as smooth as my cheek, its touch so tender and smooth, so secret and whole.

I placed the egg into my basket, on the green grass inside my basket and it remains there now in my memory, lavender on a green nest, and the memory of my little selfless self contemplating it remains there too, and the quiet beneath the soaring tree remains, still there in my memory with the lavender egg.

Now over seventy years have passed from that moment to this and it is Easter again and I know more, I know that Jesus made Easter by dying on a tree like the countless trillions of leaves that die and sail down between the trees and crumble into dirt and into the dark of the ground, and that the wetness of rain draws them down to the roots where they wait like Jesus until Easter comes and a little boy no bigger than that sees a glint of lavender appearing from the dark, from the fecund dark, from Jesus' cave, resurrecting into the little boy's hand, touching smooth against his cheek like a kiss from his mother.

Snowing God

I HAD MY FIRST ENCOUNTER WITH what people call God when I was four years old. The story may make you smile. You may even have a similar one.

There had been a snowstorm and my big brother and I went sledding. The long afternoon turned into evening. My brother told me he was cold and was going home, and that I should follow as quickly as I could. Then he disappeared up the quarter mile road to our house, pulling the sled.

It was still snowing, big gentle flakes. I was a little guy and it was a long way for me to go through the deep snow, and it was nearly dark. My mother had dressed me in a snowsuit, but I was very cold — my fingers were wet and freezing in my mittens, my toes stinging. And I had to pee very badly. I waddled along as fast as I could, the snow above my knees. I became increasingly anxious, since it would have been babyish to wet my pants, my mother would scold me, and my brother would make fun of me, but I wasn't able to unzip my snowsuit.

I came to a stone wall that was at a right angle to the path — there were large bushes in front of it making a dark tunnel between the bushes and the wall. I was desperate. I pushed through the snow into that tunnel and fell backwards into its softness.

Everything became quiet. My hood stopped making noise in my ears. Snow drifted through the branches of the bushes above me, sparkling from the light of the streetlamps out on the road. I let go. I let myself pee. The most delicious, warm feeling spread through me. I went from desperation to bliss. Suddenly everything felt enormously holy, like God was appearing in that glistening bush, though I doubt I had ever heard the word "God." I felt an all-enveloping Motherliness holding me in that moment, peaceful and warm, a Mother who was everywhere, a Mother who had no name, not my real mother but a Bigger-Than-Everything-Mother in whose presence I was completely loved and accepted. I was Home in a Home that felt so familiar — it wasn't strange at all. I knew this Place. It was so big and so close at the same time, and so loving, and the light on the falling snowflakes seemed like little sparkling angels.

Then it got cold and I struggled home.

It's tempting to think the experience of that four-year-old boy in the snow was just a matter of a physical release and the momentary comfort that followed. I can only reply that after seventy years have passed, the authenticity of that memory is still alive in me — not the physical sensations, but a numinous quality that escapes all telling. I didn't make it up. I couldn't. I was far too young and inexperienced to have any concept of holiness; I had never been to a church or been told about anything approaching that exquisite beauty or the love it radiated. And although I could, in a way, "see" it — which made it seem other than me — what I was seeing was simultaneously *inside* me — I was lit from within and without.

The soul of that little boy was touched by the remembrance of where it came from. I see now how the arc of my life has been shaped by that remembrance, or at least how it invited in time many other similar, and more intense, experiences — through psychedelics, Sufi teachings and practice, solitude in the desert, and immersion in Buddhist, Christian, Advaita, Dzogchen, and shamanic traditions. Each of these pathways to the numinous led me through different territories, yet each one ultimately revealed the same glimpse of Home, or what shall we call it? Divine love? Peace? The All-Good? Bliss? For me, to become certain that we are held by and are one with infinite love is the most beautiful teaching and gift we can receive here on earth.

Beauty Will Save
the World

WHEN I WAS YOUNG I'D WATCH my mother preparing lunches every morning for about thirty black kids who went to a free pre-school near us. Their families had scarcely enough money to feed their children, so my mother raised money or used her own to buy the bread and peanut butter, the eggs and mayonnaise and milk for their lunches. The house would fill with the smell of cookies baking early in the mornings. Then she'd pack it all in cardboard boxes, carry them down the back steps, put them into the trunk of her car and drive off to the school. She'd feed the kids, wipe their noses, sing little songs to them, and then drive home. She didn't make a big deal out of it.

When I remember those scenes — my mother's hands buttering the slices of bread all laid out in pairs on the counter, or lifting the boxes into the trunk of her car — *I feel their beauty* — there is no other way to say it. How beautiful were her simple, honest movements! I don't mean beauty in the sense of pleasing appearance, but something both within and beyond appearance. Goodness.

Plotinus said it well: "There is no beauty more real than the goodness one sees in someone."

My mother died many years ago, and yet — how wonderful! — this feeling of her beautiful selfless offering, this goodness which wasn't actually "hers" but was something greater which she gave herself to, is alive now and resonates in the world.

I know if my mother, a practical woman, could hear me talk like this, she'd give me a look and tell me to help carry the boxes. She wasn't trying to save the world; she was just doing what she could because she could.

But the beauty I'm pointing to in her actions *did* save the world. It's what always does. For me, this is the meaning of Dostoevsky's enigmatic line, *"Beauty will save the world."* Recognizing this good beauty in the actions of people around us, we are touched by a force that transcends the outer forms of what we usually think of as "beautiful." Indeed, those more tangible forms of beauty first trained us in beauty's mystery and power, and continue to do so. But they hold the potential to lead us to an even more profound recognition of the possibilities of human evolution and the human spirit.

I realize that using words such as "beauty" and "goodness" in these nervous and cynical times risks being dismissed as mere sentiment and superficiality. Our culture is entranced by the fearsome, and has come to value a tough-minded realism and even pessimism as more reliable ways to negotiate through life.

But if healing from the dark condition of human selfishness is to come, it will not come from that kind of contraction.

I believe most of us can recognize in our experience the "beautiful goodness" I'm pointing to. It doesn't mean that the people who have revealed it to us (or even ourselves) are always beautiful and good. We rise to it, and fall, and rise again. My point is that this very beauty, and the goodness that is its source, is what heals and "saves" the world, and that we can take heart in that truth. It *is* true — the Good, the True, the Beautiful. We can have faith in it, for it is ultimately of cosmic proportions —what some have called the Divine Breath that continually brings everything into being.

But to come back down to earth, and to the image of my mother buttering that bread, I'll end here with the words of a grace she liked for us to sing on festive occasions. It's sung to the melody of "We Shall Overcome."

All our food is good today,
all of life is good today,
everything that is is good today.
The future is open for us to create
so let us all give thanks today.

Letter to a
Newborn Girl

LITTLE ONE,

I've just had a letter from your father telling me that, although you were born two weeks ago, you still have not been given a name. How wonderful! You come fresh from the place where names are not needed, and it's good that you can carry that quietness about you a little while longer. In that place there's a blissful secret most of us can no longer remember. I think we would bow at your feet if you could tell us about it, if you could remind us what we have forgotten, but of course, you do not know words yet and that's just how you remain wiser and holy and inscrutable to us.

But soon you will start to learn words. You will learn to say what you feel and want, and with that saying you too will forget what is so natural to you now. Or perhaps you will be lucky, and a current of the bliss you come from will continue to stream through your heart — I pray it will! This world you have arrived into is a serious place, often tragic, and remembering the beauty of your origin can be a great help in the years to come.

I'm an old man now and I have a lifetime of experiences behind me; you, you've just hatched out of the egg and are as innocent as the morning! Because of that, I suppose it's only natural that I should want to give you some advice that I hope might make things easier for you as your life unfolds. I know advice from one's elders can be tedious, and even a little pointless, considering that each of us is unique and each of us has to find our own way. So I'll just name five lessons here that have served me well in my own life, and you can do with them what you wish.

Know you are safe. That's the first lesson and for me it's been the bedrock of my life. When I've been uncertain, when I've been afraid, when accidents have happened, I've somehow been reassured deep down that all shall be well. Even though "knowing I am safe" has mostly supported me in the mundane challenges of my life, it has ultimately freed me from the fear of death, which is no small thing in the drama of being a mortal. We're safe. Everything is all right forever. We are made out of light. I think you know that yourself now, as the infant without a name that you are. One day you may doubt it — that's part of the drama — but if you remember nothing else from this letter, I hope that, when things get rough, you will remember this: *know you are safe.*

Here's another lesson that's been dear to my life: *Walk in the open air.* That's a way of saying spend as much time as you can in nature, in the open air, in places that humans have not built on and paved over. The natural world will teach you, heal you, and replenish your soul with its beauty. It is, like you are now, fresh from the generosity of the Unnamable. When your love for wild nature is alive in you, you will find it is an inexhaustible source for your creativity and for your caring for others and this beautiful planet. *Walk in the open air.*

Another: *Pretend you can do it.* I know that sounds a little odd, but I can only tell you it's been the way I've learned all my life and how I've managed to do things I never imagined I could. One day you'll hold a pencil in your hand and you'll want to draw a tree — just pretend you can do it and start drawing. Or you'll kiss a boy for the first time — pretend you can do it. Or you'll be asked to lead a meeting and you've never done that before — just pretend you can do it. Of course, you'll make mistakes, your fingers will miss notes on the piano, but just try again, "pretending" or believing you can do it, and slowly by slowly you'll learn how.

One more: *Be interested in everything.* Be a generalist. Neglect nothing that is part of life. Be curious and amazed by things. Listen to others. Welcome new ways of seeing, but always think for yourself. Gain skills that have nothing to do with each other, like repairing a broken chair, fasting in the wilderness, speaking Portuguese, consoling people in distress, singing. As societies get more stressed in the years ahead because of climate change and the host of dangers facing us, being a generalist will serve you and others well.

Lastly — and I name it last because it's the most resistant to description — *Follow your love.* Do what you love. Love what you love. I can't say that love will protect you from mistakes or sorrow — it hasn't done that for me — but in its mysterious way it makes everything worthwhile. I'm not talking simply about love that's affection or passion — although it's that too — but love that continually moves to heal what is broken or has been separated. Follow that. This world you have come into is full of hurt and distrust and density (as well as beauty!), and your love is the gift that will heal it.

Little one, you are starting on a great adventure. Follow your love. Be interested in everything. Pretend you can do it. Walk in the open air. Know you are safe.

A Hundred Years
from Now

THERE ARE INCREASING SIGNS THAT A hundred years from now life on earth will have taken a serious turn for the worse. We won't be here of course, but our grandchildren and great-grandchildren will. What will they have to face?

Thinking of the future with grim expectations like this can be disturbing and scary, like imagining the sword of Damocles swinging from a thread above us. We've started having bad dreams about what might happen — visions of nations collapsing, citizens armed and dangerous, the coasts flooding, forests burning, dust blowing over dried-out farmland, starving refugees taking what they can find, the last elephants shot for meat, the seas dying, dystopian mega-cities swarming with faceless strangers, replicants, sex robots, aimless wars fought for nothing.... We keep dreaming these things. We see them beginning now and we hate ourselves for what we're doing.

I want to be able to say it's not too late. I want to believe that these dreams, becoming every day more real, will scare us awake and with the shock of waking we will remember what matters to us and what kind of world we want to leave for our children, and theirs, and theirs.

But even in waking, the dark dreams linger. We feel powerless, too insignificant to effect the changes that are needed. That's one of the dreams too, our powerlessness. But like the rest of our anxious dreams, it doesn't have to be true. We're *not* powerless.

I've spent much of my life working on projects for positive social change — practical, grassroots efforts in cooperation with others — and this kind of citizen-activist work is an essential part of the power we have. But I want to point here to a deeper power, a power without which all of our hard work would be aimless and short-lived, a power that each of us has right now and can put to use at any time.

Behind every act of kindness, behind every plea for justice, behind every move we make to take apart the structures of violence that undergird human societies, there is something clear and luminous. That clear luminosity is our love, our love for what matters to us. It's what we stand for; it's what gets us on our feet, again and again. It's not exactly an emotion; it's deeper than that. Ultimately it's not even about loving specific things that matter to us — it includes that, but goes beyond. Love itself is what matters. It's the very current of life arising in and through us, and is at the heart of whatever power we have to heal the world.

I realize this begins to sound blurry and impractical — words like "love" can do that. We've become accustomed to thinking that only actions that produce measurable change in the "real world" will make a difference. As someone with a practical bent myself, I can appreciate that sentiment. But the longer I live the more I sense there are other realities or "energies" at work shaping what happens. What we call "love" is one of them, perhaps the most important.

I've come to believe that the more we love, the more love lives in the world. We might think of love as a kind of light that radiates from us, an invisible light with the power to penetrate and leaven the density of the world. If this is true, then we are not powerless. Even if our life situation doesn't allow us to become actively engaged in service of some sort, we can serve. We can love.

What does that mean? What can we love? My feeling is it doesn't much matter what we love, we just need to love what we love. We need to keep discovering what that is. For example, we could start close in, discovering the love we feel for the warmth of our bodies, or our love for our breathing, or for our capacity to see. We can love the simple things of the world, love the way morning light spreads across the breakfast table, love the feel of our feet on a path, love the company of a dear friend or the sound of children at play. Love all the people we meet today, despite their flaws. We can sit under a tree and love the roots and branches and the sky. Love the babies being born right now, love their mothers, love their fathers, love everyone who will help them throughout their lives. Love the people near and far who are suffering, who are oppressed, whose lives are hurt by other people's selfishness and fear. Love all the kindness everywhere, the generosity and self-sacrifice. Love the miracle of loving it-self. As Sufi teacher Fazal Inayat-Khan said, "You can always love more."

Imagine that every moment we love, we are enlivening the world with that love. The world gets lighter, freer, because of our loving. Imagine that love is a current that can warm the heart of things, that can dispel the density and ignorance of the dark futures we fear. Love is a living force, a power, even when it is does not seem to energize specific action.

We live in anxious times, and there is no denying the storm clouds that are gathering around us. I am not suggesting we ignore that reality. I am simply saying that the future world depends on our keeping the flame of our love burning. Even if our bad dreams come to pass and the world has to endure that long darkness, if the flame of our love is still burning it will help guide our descendants onward.

I remember a moment that occurred several years ago that touched me deeply with this lesson. I was in Gaza, interviewing a Hamas leader and others as part of my work with a project called the Nonviolent Peaceforce (www.nonviolentpeaceforce. org). Even though I was prepared for it, the condition of life for the million and a half people locked in that small piece of land shocked me. Blasted buildings, warrens of little streets strewn with trash, extreme poverty, and a pervading sense of despair. It was our bad dreams manifest.

By the time I left Gaza, driving up the coast road in a beat-up taxi, I was thoroughly depressed. And then, as I gazed out the taxi window, something up in the air caught my eye. It was a kite!

Brightly colored, dancing in the shore wind. Then I saw another, and another. Children on the beach were flying kites! Suddenly that vision of kites flying up from the dismal conditions of Gaza blew through my depression. My heart took a breath. I saw that as long as the children fly kites in the free air, as long as their love for the wind and the kites and the play and each other is alive, there is hope.

> *Lovers find secret places inside this violent world*
> *where they make transactions with beauty.*
>
> *Reason says, Nonsense.*
> *I have walked and measured the walls here.*
> *There are no places like that.*
>
> *Love says, There are.*
>
> — *Rumi*

How to Survive the
Apocalypse

- *Wake up early*
- *Get out of your way*
- *Unlock your doors*
- *Share what you have*
- *Don't try to put the world back to the way it was*
- *Ask for help*
- *Complain less, love more*
- *Stay steady*
- *Trade, don't steal*
- *Do what is obvious*
- *Take zoo animals back to their homes*
- *Tear down tall buildings*
- *Don't be rich*
- *Don't follow orders*
- *Make music without electricity*

LOVE'S DRUM

- *Play without keeping score*
- *Get your hands dirty*
- *Work next to children*
- *Protect libraries*
- *Live lean*
- *Don't worry about dying*
- *Pretend the air is God*
- *Feed the ground*
- *Pray into moving water*
- *Build temples in forests*
- *In the evenings tell good stories*
- *Give America back to the Indians*
- *Pay reparations, never enough*
- *Don't make gunpowder*
- *Don't be smug*
- *Love anyone you want*
- *Make things beautiful this time*
- *Add to this list*

A New Year's Vow

Because this day is special
and we are together,
because the year's starting
and we want to say something,
because it's never been here before
and we have,
because the year is asking
and the children are asking and listening
for what we will say
and what we will do,
let us vow, let us make a vow,
now, because we can,
because we're still breathing,
and the old year hurt,
and the animals are anxious,
and the children are waiting,
and the air is listening,

let us vow, now,
to the mothers who bore us
and the millenniums before us
and the millenniums to come
who are waiting and listening
for what we will say
and what we will do,
and because it matters
and we are together,
let us vow, now,
to love more.

~

A Prayer in the Militant Mosque — 2010

The Mosque

The dawn call to prayer wakes me. It is still dark in Islamabad. Half dreaming I imagine the notes of the praying man's song rise up through the neighborhood like a line of thin silver leaves, finding their way along the streets, brushing against closed doors, against windows, sliding through cracks into rooms, touching the skin of sleeping people like me, waking us if we are ready. *Hayya 'ala-salat! – Come to pray!*

While I am not formally a Muslim, I am not formally anything — and this gives me the chance to join praying people wherever they are. I get out of bed, dress, and leave the hotel into the still dark city. The sleepy guards at the gate with their submachine guns straighten up and nod to me as I go out.

There are no cars. An old turbaned street sweeper moves bits of paper along the gutter with his twig broom.

The *Lal Masjid* — the Red Mosque — is surrounded by a fence topped with razor wire, but the gate is wide open. I leave my shoes at the door.

An entry area opens onto a large, dimly lit prayer hall planted with columns; a few small lights break the shadows. Prayers are about to start. I join the line of about fifty men, shoulder to shoulder, waiting. One of the parts I like best about Muslim prayers is this line in which everyone is accepted equally — although I am obviously not Pakistani and look very different from everyone else, it doesn't seem to matter. I also love when we touch our foreheads to the ground — the thought-filled heads of us men grounded on the common earth like electrical wires, for this moment subdued.

After prayers half the men leave. Those who remain sit in a corner listening to a lesson from a quiet-spoken teacher standing amidst them. A few sit in the shadows praying by themselves, wrapped in their shawls like mounds of sand. The few lights are turned off and the hall becomes part of the dawn, the central dome brushed with blue-gray light. The soft sound of the teacher's mingles with the voices of the solitary men reciting their prayers. The place feels like one peaceful heart waking in the dawn.

THE BATTLE

I sit listening. I try to hear the gunshots, the whiz of bullets glancing off these columns, the shouts, death cries and weeping that filled this mosque two and a half years ago when the Pakistan army attacked the several thousand madrassa students and heavily armed militants who had barricaded themselves here.

The Red Mosque and its large compound had long been used by Pakistan's intelligence service, the ISI, as a station for organizing and training militants who were sent to Afghanistan to battle the Soviets, or to fight in Kashmir. The ISI continued to support this mosque and other Islamist training centers like it after the 9/11 attacks — on the one hand seeking to align themselves with the Taliban so they would have leverage against the increasing influence of India in Afghanistan, and on the other hand so they could continue receiving American military aid to counter the Taliban/al-Qaeda presence in their own country.

But by 2007 this strategy came back to bite them. The Red Mosque had become the center of Islamist militancy against the Pakistan state itself in the very heart of the capital. The ISI could no longer control what went on here, and ruefully could have said with Macbeth:

> ...that we but teach
> Bloody instructions, which, being taught, return
> To plague the inventor.

In July 2007, the mullahs and *talibs* (militant students) in the mosque threatened civil war if the Pakistan government did not accept Sharia law. The government, now eager to regain credibility in the eyes of the international community, reacted brutally. After the Pakistan army's first assault on the mosque, many talibs escaped. Those who remained pledged to become martyrs. The final battle lasted three days and hundreds were killed.

The fall of the Red Mosque was a turning point for Pakistan. Extremists across Pakistan banded together, determined to destroy the government and establish an Islamic state. The terrorist attacks that resulted provoked ever more violent responses from the Pakistan military, fueling an increasingly militant backlash from the population caught in the crossfire.

This particular sequence of events — a militant provocation is met with a brutal reaction from the state, which in turn causes more people to become militant, which leads to further polarization and destabilization — has been described as the basic Islamist terrorist strategy, and it is working.

The violent reactions of state powers to terrorist violence have played into the hands of the terrorists. Their long-term objective is to exhaust the will and resources of the state, creating opportunities for new Islamist regimes on local and ultimately national levels.

THE PRAYER

As I sit in the dawn light of the mosque, painfully aware of this dark tragedy, I try to pray — but everything that comes to my mind feels trite. What words could be adequate to address the suffering that took place here, and that continues around the world?

So I stop trying to pray and just sit still.

And then slowly, out of the stillness, I begin to sense something.

What is it? Tenderness? Intimacy? Whatever it is, it is not complicated at all. It is utterly simple and familiar in the same way my sense of being is familiar.

It feels to me like the very heart of prayer — but prayer without any words, without even the sense of communication from the human world to a divine one. I am not making this happen — it is here already — a simple and unmistakable sense of connection, an intimacy with everything all at once.

In this intimacy there is no sense of judgment about good or bad, right or wrong, no distance between things. Nothing is excluded — not the wounded and dying talibs in this mosque, or the mullahs trying to be Allah's heroes, or the frightened citizens in the locked-down city, or the politicians in their violent reactions, or people around the world anxious for their lives. Nothing is excluded.

It is as if a vast compassionate silence pervades our global tragedy, what Muslims call *the Merciful, the Compassionate — ir rahman ir rahim* — deep in the rock of this mosque, deep in the air between us — an unspeakable compassion holding us all.

As I leave the mosque I hear my practical self ask: So? What good is it? What good is sensing this numinous compassion when the world is so full of hatred and violence? Don't we need pragmatic policies that will liberate us from fear and the desire for dominance that poisons human history?

Yes, of course we do. But there is another pragmatism, and it feels to me that to realize and appreciate *in this place* the compassion and intimacy that connects everything is why I have come halfway around the world — why, unknown to myself, I got out of bed in the dark this morning to come here. For a few moments at least, the militancy and self-righteous fundamentalism of this place became transparent, and I became transparent with it — everything released its position — and our common intimacy was revealed.

It may be that for us to touch this prayer of our common heart, even briefly, is where we need to return, where we need to begin again, where we might finally find our way to a world of peace.

~

The Soul of the World – 2022

YOU WAKE UP WITH AN IMAGE you saw on the news yesterday: a shaky cellphone video of a Russian missile slamming into the side of an apartment building in Kyiv. You imagine the aftermath, the dangling light fixtures, the kitchen cabinets hanging on walls exposed to the day, peoples' private nests blown open for all to see. You want to stop seeing, but you can't. You imagine there's a child in a back bedroom, thrown from her bed, making her way through the debris to the kitchen doorway to find her parents. You see her smudged face looking out at the city where the kitchen used to be. But then you don't see her — for a moment *you see what she's seeing* — as if you are her, rubbing soot from your eyes.

Praise that shaky cellphone and the one who held it! Now our eyes are there too, in Kyiv and Kharkiv, on the Minneapolis asphalt with George Floyd, in Charleston, Portland, Tehran,

Moscow, Yangon. Now we are bearing witness in a new way, up close and personal even though we're safely in our homes far from the brutality and chaos. There's an immediacy and rawness to these cellphone videos — we hear the gasps and shouts of the people there, we feel them — these are people like us holding up their cellphones to the violent moment so we can witness *with* them, so we can feel that what's happening to them is also happening to us.

These humble videos (along, of course, with on-the-ground news reports from brave journalists) are a powerful force touching the souls of billions of people throughout the world. That we're disturbed by what we see, that we share a common revulsion at the senseless killing and destruction, says something about the nature of our billions of souls. To me, it says that we share a *soulness* in common, a sensitivity and reverence for life that's built-in to our being human — though for some that soul-depth is tragically occluded by fear and greed.

What is it, this soulness we share? Could it be that all our private souls are sprouts from one vast soul — *a world soul* — like a forest of individual aspen trees emerging from the same living network of roots? However we conceive it, as "soul" or "sensitivity" or "life-reverence," it reveals a mutuality of caring among us that's intensified now by the interconnectivity of our eyes. We're realizing we're not as separate as we thought. Our mutuality of caring, this inner soulness we share, is now wired outwardly in a way that's never happened before, billions of cellphones linked by a neuronal web throughout the world — inner soul and outer eyes revealing what matters to us.

But then, when we bear witness like this, watching the news reports and shaky videos far removed from the violence, we can feel impotent and useless. "I can't do anything to help!" we cry to ourselves.

Is that true? Are we helpless?

I believe the very fact that we *see* what's happening, that we bear witness together even though we can't do anything to affect the situation outwardly, is a radical form of activism. We are connecting with and deepening the evolving soul of the world. We are sensitizing the conscience of humanity. Though it may seem insignificant, our dismay with bombs dropping on Ukrainian cities is a powerful action. Without it, without our caring, the human spirit would be diminished.

Even though it hurts to bear witness like this, even though we want to turn away, our anonymous solidarity with those who are suffering, wherever they are and whoever they may be, ennobles the vast soul of the world and makes possible the coming of peace.

Autumn Light

for Pierre Delattre

Walking through a park you pass an old man sitting on a bench. He's watching children out on the grass playing and tumbling in the fallen leaves. You see the wrinkles and lines in his old face as you pass. What kind of life carved those lines? Hieroglyphics of stories even he probably can't remember. On a whim you sit on a bench down the path across from him, and wait.

You wonder about him. He just sits there watching the children, or looking up into the trees. You wonder what he's thinking. Is he thinking? Maybe not. Does he have ambitions? Does he make plans?

A little breeze scatters leaves along the path, and more leaves flutter down from the branches to join them. You wonder what it's like to be old. You decide to pretend you're as old as he is, with the majority of your life behind you — just another old person on a bench in a park somewhere on an autumn afternoon.

You imagine first that being old must feel a little cranky, that you'll be annoyed that your youth has passed and that your body hurts and no one cares about you. But then you look over at the old man and notice he has a slight smile on his lips. He doesn't look cranky, if anything he looks contented.

So you try feeling that way, contented. You put the same slight smile on your lips. You look lazily out across the park. A thought comes up about your next appointment, but you know the appointment is still two hours from now, plenty of time, and you already know what needs to be accomplished when the time comes. Other thoughts float by but you're an old person now and you just pretend those thoughts don't matter. They're not really interesting anyway.

You invite yourself to feel fine just sitting there with nothing needing to be done. Just sitting, enjoying the autumn light sifting through the trees. At first it feels a little odd, this sitting quietly without the familiar pressure of wanting to distract yourself or get the next thing done. But you keep on with the experiment, letting yourself feel old, contented and at ease.

And then something extraordinary happens, all by itself. You couldn't explain it if you tried. It's as if the space *between* things goes right *through* things, right through you and the park and the old man and the children playing. You sense a spaciousness and closeness that's so familiar it feels like it's you, and yet it's everywhere, completely empty of anything and yet full of everything at the same time. And the autumn light is just the same — the slant of the sun seems like it's passing through your body and through the trees and the ground, as if everything is transparent even though everything's right here too.

And there's something else, something even more intimate. The familiar place that's felt like the "you" inside of you, the you behind your eyes, the place of you that agrees with itself and quarrels with itself and makes judgments about everything, that place is suddenly so sweetly quiet and wide open and transparent too, just like space. You've never felt anything like this before. There's an expansiveness everywhere that's so vast and at the same time so intimate and lovely. It feels like you're in love with everything! Your heart has burst open. The enormity of what you're feeling is so unexpected and beautiful that you wonder if you're going crazy.

You look down the path at the old man on his bench and see he's looking at you. He winks.

Love and Death

Lying there, looking up at the doctor and your next of kin, you grow uncomfortable with their concerned faces. You close your eyes so they will think you need to rest. You hear them back out of the room and the soft click of the door. You can still hear them speaking out in the hall, most of the words indecipherable except for the doctor's, who you distinctly hear say, "It won't be long now."

It sounds like a line from a movie you saw once — *it won't be long now* — but this time it's about you. Ah, so this is my death-bed. The words form again in your mind, "my death-bed," and again, "my death-bed," as if repeating them will make you believe it's true. My time has come. A quiver of fear — or is it excitement? — flashes in your stomach, but it doesn't last. You lie there without moving. It's quiet in your room. You're thankful they brought you home; the hospital with its noises and interruptions wasn't a good place to die.

You feel wide-awake, but as you cast your mind over the history of your life, letting images from different periods arise, you fall into a half-dream state and drift. Gradually you sense a presence close to you, although no one has come into the room. It's not a presence you can identify, but it feels somehow familiar. Kind. Is it an angel? It's asking you something. You strain to hear it, and then the words become clear.

"Have you loved well?" it asks. That's all, nothing more.

You hear the question echoing down the corridors of your life, doors opening on moments you're sure bear witness to your failure to love. You know this feeling, this old feeling of unworthiness, of having failed somehow. No, I haven't loved well, certainly not well enough, good God all the times I was self-preoccupied instead of loving, impatient instead of gentle, oh God…

You feel the weight of judgment — your own, the angel's, God's — fall on you like shovelfuls of earth, darkening and compressing against you. You strain to breathe. But now in the darkness you sense something else — at first it's faint, then unmistakable — it's the smell of earth, the smell of soil in a garden where you once knelt, the dark, loamy, sweet smell of fertile soil breathing into you. How lovely it is!

Now chinks of light appear beneath you — it's strange, there's light beneath you and you feel yourself falling into it, but suddenly everything turns around and what felt like down a moment ago is now up, and you're looking up into blue sky and as you breathe it feels like you're breathing in the whole wide sky, clear and fresh. How lovely it is!

There are a few puffy white clouds balanced in the sky, precious against the blue. Two birds glide over the landscape. You hear leaves whispering in the trees. So beautiful!

Now you are walking. There's the familiar stride of your body along the path, confident that it knows how to adjust each step around the small stones and the tilt of the ground. You remember this, how beautiful it is to walk, to feel yourself glide along past the trunks of trees, how lovely it is!

Suddenly it all becomes clear to you: the enormous gift your life has been, all the moments given you to love — the wonder of it! — to have received this chance to breathe this air, to walk in this body on the earth. Gratitude wells up in your heart: Oh yes, I have loved this!

Now you are no longer walking, now images as real as life are passing through you, images from your earliest memories, flashes of wonder in your child eyes, your mother picking you up, oh! riding your bike through leaves fluttering down around you, the images that come are as numerous as those falling leaves, tying your shoelace for the first time and looking up smiling, holding your first friend's hand, kissing, that feeling of soft lips kissing yours, two hearts kissing, how I have loved this! And each tender, shy love I have taken in my arms, each one, each one loved, longed for, each one! Images of love pour through you in a great current of gratitude, alleluias of white birds flying up, images of stairways, carrying groceries, cooking dinner, children playing under the table, their laughter and nonsense talk, oh how I have loved this! And laying my head on my pillow so many times, its touch on my cheek, the open window in the morning billowing the curtain, the smell of coffee brewing, music from a neighbor's radio, sunlight on the porch. I remember! The images continue, beyond telling, and your heart feels like it's bursting with gladness. You feel yourself coming apart as if a child was blowing on a dandelion puff. You want to say something, one last shout to everyone everywhere, one last whisper in everyone's ear as you come apart, you want to say, *Love well! Love well!*

When they come back into your room they see you lying there, a little smile on your lips, very still.

I Only Want to Say

NOW THAT I AM OLD MY thoughts no longer hold the certainty they had, instead they open like a river delta does, spreading to the sea, slow calm channels where grasses bow and water birds float and dive and make their homes. The torrent of my beliefs has eased, thank God, and I no longer need to convince anyone of anything. You and they will find your way. I only want to say how good it is and how good you are, as you try to make things better, how good it is that this is the way it is, and that we are not alone and never were, the same water flowing to the sea and lifting us to the clouds. It is beautiful that we have been made like this, out of mud and air, made so finely that our eyes can shine with the dearest love. There is nothing to be afraid of. This may be the best, the most important job we have: to assure one another that each of us is loveable, and that mercy softens every fall. Death, after all, is a fine homecoming. As I age and slow I wonder if my life has any meaning left. It does! Meaning beyond the need for meaning, this one that drenches me with thankfulness.

I am not at war with a meaningless void. There is no need for meaning, here where we glisten like raindrops in the sunlight, each drop a prism. Something unspeakably good is shining here, some generosity so quiet and nonchalant it leaves no trace of itself yet appears as you and me and every moment created and left behind, nothing ever personal yet everything always intimate. Mountains slide into the sea, even oceans wave goodbye, and we are not what we seem. My mother died and poured herself into my emptiness. My father followed. I join them, even now. So shall we walk together, you and I, and watch the evening sky turn into stars? Shall we talk together about what we think is happening? It doesn't matter if what we say is true. God after all is too holy to know, and we can be content to say *our hearts have no edge* and leave it at that. Look how we are made of the warmest light! It loves us without any words.

Permissions

Page 7: "The barzakh is *between-between*..." From ©1998 William C Chittick, *The Self-Disclosure of God, Principles of Al-Arabi's Cosmology*. Reprinted with permission from SUNY Press, suny-press.edu.

Page 8: "...And these Things, which live by perishing..." "The Ninth Elegy," translation copyright © 1982 by Stephen Mitchell; from *Selected Poetry of Rainer Maria Rilke*, edited and translated by Stephen Mitchell. Used by permission of Random House, an imprint and division of Penguin Random House LLC. All rights reserved.

Page 13: "In the uncertain light of single, certain truth..." "Notes Toward a Supreme Fiction," copyright © 1942 by Wallace Stevens; from *The Collected Poems of Wallace Stevens* by Wallace Stevens. Used by permission of Alfred A. Knopf, an imprint of the Knopf

Page 20: "If there is pain, it is this:" From ©2012 William C. Chittick, *In Search of the Lost Heart, Explorations in Islamic Thought*. Reprinted with permission from SUNY Press, sunypress.edu.

Page 34: "It was the womb itself, aloneness, alaya vijnana..." Jack Kerouac, excerpt from #64 from *The Scripture of the Golden Eternity*. Copyright © 1960, 1970, 1994 by Jan Kerouac and Anthony Sampatakakos. Reprinted with the permission of The Permissions Company, LLC on behalf of City Lights Books, www.citylights.com.

Page 46: "And the truth is..." From English translation © 2011 David Henry Wilson, original text © 1990 Suhrkamp Verlag, Hermann Hesse, *Hymn to Old Age* (translated by David Wilson). Reprinted with permission from Pushkin Press, pushkinpress. com.

Page 108: "In order to have warm human relations..." From ©1998 Dainin Katagiri, *You Have to Say Something*. Shambhala Publications, Inc

Page 120: "Love is the mark of the Tribe..." From ©2013 William C. Chittick, *Divine Love, Islamic Literature and the Path to God*.

Reprinted with permission from Yale University Press, yale-books.yale.edu.

ABOUT THE AUTHOR

Pir Elias Amidon is the spiritual director (Pir) of the Sufi Way (www.sufiway.org), a contemporary and non-sectarian inner school in the lineage of Sufi Inayat Khan. Pir Elias teaches and holds retreats on nondual spirituality and Sufism throughout Europe and the United States, and is known for his direct and experiential approach to spiritual realization. For over two decades Elias led vision quests with his wife, Elizabeth Roberts, in the deserts of Utah, Spain, and the forests of northern Thailand. He also worked for many years in the field of peace and environmental activism in the Middle East and Southeast Asia, and with indigenous tribes on land-rights issues. He is the author of *The Open Path: Recognizing Nondual Awareness; Free Medicine:*

Meditations on Nondual Awakening; Munajat: Forty Prayers, and *The Book of Flashes,* and co-editor with Elizabeth of the three anthologies *Earth Prayers, Life Prayers,* and *Prayers for a Thousand Years.*

For information about the Sufi Way and its current programs visit *www.sufiway.org.*

Sentient Publications, LLC publishes nonfiction books on cultural creativity, experimental education, transformative spirituality, holistic health, new science, ecology, and other topics, approached from an integral viewpoint. We also publish fiction that aims to intrigue, stimulate, and entertain. Our authors are intensely interested in exploring the nature of life from fresh perspectives, addressing life's great questions, and fostering the full expression of the human potential. Sentient Publications' books arise from the spirit of inquiry and the richness of the inherent dialogue between writer and reader.

Our Culture Tools series is designed to give social catalyzers and cultural entrepreneurs the essential information, technology, and inspiration to forge a sustainable, creative, and compassionate world.

We are very interested in hearing from our readers. To direct suggestions or comments to us, or to be added to our mailing list, please contact:

SENTIENT PUBLICATIONS, LLC

PO Box 1851
Boulder, CO 80306
303-443-2188
contact@sentientpublications.com
www.sentientpublications.com